Cut Loose

Break the Rules of Scrapbooking

by Crystal Jeffrey Rieger

MEMORY
MAKERS
BOOKS

Cincinnati, Ohio

www.mycraftivity.com

About the Author

* Crystal Jeffrey Rieger

Crystal Jeffrey Rieger has always been interested in art, which she trained in for years before moving on to the world of fashion. After the birth of her son, she decided to stay home, and when the need for creativity set in, she went in search for something to do. She soon found scrapbooking and it was love at first sight. A year later she was selected as a 2007 Memory Makers Master and she has been happily creating and writing for Memory Makers ever since. She currently maintains a blog at www.memorymakersmagazine.com/crystaljeffreyrieger. She lives in Canada with her husband and two kids on a beautiful horse farm.

Cut Loose! Copyright© 2008 by Crystal Jeffrey Rieger. Manufactured in China. All rights reserved. It is permissible for the purchaser to make the projects contained herein and sell them at fairs, bazaars and craft shows. No other part of this book may be reproduced in any form or by any electronic or mechanical means including information storage and retrieval systems without permission in writing from the publisher, except by a reviewer, who may quote a brief passage in review. Published by Memory Makers Books, an imprint of F+W Publications, Inc., 4700 East Galbraith Road, Cincinnati, Ohio 45236. (800) 289-0963. First edition.

12 11 10 09 08   5 4 3 2 1

Distributed in Canada by Fraser Direct
100 Armstrong Avenue
Georgetown, ON, Canada L7G 5S4
Tel: (905) 877-4411

Distributed in the U.K. and Europe by David & Charles
Brunel House, Newton Abbot, Devon, TQ12 4PU, England
Tel: (+44) 1626 323200, Fax: (+44) 1626 323319
E-mail: postmaster@davidandcharles.co.uk

Distributed in Australia by Capricorn Link
P.O. Box 704, S. Windsor, NSW 2756 Australia
Tel: (02) 4577-3555

Library of Congress Cataloging-in-Publication Data

Rieger, Crystal Jeffrey.
  Cut loose! : break the rules of scrapbooking / Crystal Jeffrey Rieger. – 1st ed.
    p. cm.
  Includes index.
  ISBN 978-1-59963-020-5 (pbk. : alk. paper)
  1. Photograph albums. 2. Photographs–Conservation and restoration. 3. Scrapbooks. I. Title.
TR465.R52 2008
745.593–dc22
                        2007048287

fw
F+W PUBLICATIONS, INC.
www.fwpublications.com

Metric Conversion Chart

to convert →	to →	multiply by
Inches	Centimeters	2.54
Centimeters	Inches	0.4
Feet	Centimeters	30.5
Centimeters	Feet	0.03
Yards	Meters	0.9
Meters	Yards	1.1
Sq. Inches	Sq. Centimeters	6.45
Sq. Centimeters	Sq. Inches	0.16
Sq. Feet	Sq. Meters	0.09
Sq. Meters	Sq. Feet	10.8
Sq. Yards	Sq. Meters	0.8
Sq. Meters	Sq. Yards	1.2
Pounds	Kilograms	0.45
Kilograms	Pounds	2.2
Ounces	Grams	28.3
Grams	Ounces	0.035

Editor: Kristin Boys
Designer: Kelly O'Dell
Art Coordinator: Eileen Aber
Production Coordinator: Matt Wagner
Photographers: Melanie Warner, Tim Grondin, Christine Polomsky
Stylist: Nora Martini

Dedication

To **Austin**, for all the sacrifices you made so this book was possible, for all the encouragement you gave me throughout the process and, most of all, for loving me no matter what. I dedicate this book to you, my husband, the love of my life.

Acknowledgments

* Writing a book is not something you do alone. It is unbelievable how many people have touched this book in some way, and I am forever in their debt (though I would have appreciated their company during the long nights it took to write this!).

* First I have to acknowledge my kidlets, Harper and Magnus. I am so lucky to have you both. Who would have guessed that I would end up with both the cutest girl and the cutest boy in the entire world! I am pretty lucky indeed. Thank you for providing so much fodder for my pages; they just wouldn't be the same without you. I love you both. I must also acknowledge my family: my mom, my dad, my sisters and brother and their spouses who have all, at times, had to listen to me talk about scrapbooking and have always been supportive in whatever I have done. This means the world to me.

* I cannot write a book and not mention Nicole, who has been a friend like no other, a friend who understood me disappearing for months during the creation of this book—and is still speaking to me. I also have to put into writing: Come home, I miss you! I must also thank Ronee Parsons, because without the push she gave and the support she offered, this book would not exist. She is an amazing woman who I am proud to call a friend. I also want to thank the contributors to this book, Anilu, Erin, Janine, Jeniece, Michelle and Ronee. You women are amazing and rose to this challenge beautifully. Thank you for stepping out of your comfort zones and creating the beautiful art that graces the pages of this book. I have enjoyed working with every one of you, and the book is so much better because of you.

* I have to say thank you to Christine Doyle, who helped me through the beginning of this book and was so open to this idea. Thank you for giving me this opportunity. I also must give a great big thanks to Kristin Boys, my editor. I never realized before why authors thanked their editors so profusely, but now I know! Thank you for being so great to work with and ultimately making this book and me look good. Your patience over the months has been much appreciated. Last, but certainly not least, I have to thank F+W for giving me the chance to write this book and for the Memory Makers staff for believing in me. Thank you. It has all been a dream come true.

CONTENTS

INTRODUCTION

Life is full of rules, and scrapbooking is no exception. Rules are great. They provide guidelines for our pages, and they help us become comfortable as we learn our craft. But they can quickly become boundaries that stifle our creativity. By trying to follow the rules all the time, you cut yourself off to possibilities. Scrapbooking is a creative hobby, which means there is no right and wrong way to do it. There are no scrapbooking police. No one is going to tell you your scrapbook layout is not a real layout because you did not follow "the rules."

This book is meant to open your eyes to all the rules you follow, consciously or not. With tons of examples of how to break the rules, this book is bound to spark a bit of a rebel in you and get you creating in fresh new ways. Being a rule rebel doesn't mean that your scrapbook pages need to be completely out there. Like me, you probably still want your pages to look like scrapbook layouts. I want my photos to be recognizable, my journaling to be clear and my memories and thoughts to be preserved. You can accomplish all this and still be a rule breaker. This book is meant to stretch you creatively, not change the way you scrap completely. Follow me as I show you ways to push yourself past the rules. I'll give you a nudge down a path that you might not have gone down otherwise.

As you go through this book and try some of the challenges, you may find that not everything is for you. You may find that adding elements on an angle takes you too far out of your comfort zone, but you may also find that choosing colors with different intensities gives you the creative kick you need. I hope that as you become aware of the rules, try the challenges and look through the book for inspiration, you will start to create with a greater sense of freedom and find what works for you.

Sure, there is a time and place for rules. But sometimes you need to cut loose so you can give yourself true creative freedom. Remember, the only "should" in scrapbooking is you should have fun!

chapter

grace

i worry about

light in the darkness

FABULOUS FUNDAMENTALS:
The Basic Rules of Scrapbooking

The basics of scrapbooking are the rules you learn in the beginning. They are trusted friends and they make you feel secure. Over and over, the basics offer a solid foundation from which to create pages. These rules become so ingrained that you give them no thought when you sit down to create. Sound familiar? These basic rules are good. But they are safe. And when you stay within the boundaries, it's easy for monotony to creep in. So, it's time to get out of your comfort zone and kick things up a bit. By making just a few simple changes to your routine, you can make your pages can look fresh again. Take it one fundamental at a time, and before you know it, you'll be a true rule breaker.

1 RULE

Every scrapbook page needs a title, photo and journaling

All "good" scrapbook pages contain the golden three: a title, photo and journaling. You have been inundated with this rule, right? But sometimes a title seems redundant to your page. Or you don't have photos that contribute to your story. Or you have a photo that speaks more clearly than any journaling could. Don't get me wrong: This rule is a rule for a good reason. Using a title, photos and journaling often helps convey your complete story. But these elements are not mandatory. No one is going to tell you your page is not a real scrapbook page just because you didn't include the golden three.

Magnus 1. Summer '06

THE REASON I ♥ BEING MOM

I wanted the focus of this layout to be this favorite photo I had captured of my son and me. The photo speaks a very clear message to me, and with one short phrase I am able to communicate it to the viewer. Using a large font for the journaling phrase allows it to act visually as the title, making the page feel complete.

Supplies: Patterned paper (Hambly, Scenic Route); transparency (Hambly); clear shapes (Heidi Swapp); felt flower (Dollarstore); label sticker (Papier Valise); ribbon (Michaels); rhinestones (Westrim); tags (Every Jot & Tittle);
Misc: adhesive, floss, letter stickers, paint, pen, trim

YOUR CHALLENGE
Use one short message that acts as both a title and your journaling on a scrapbook page.

Artwork by Michelle Guray

Even without journaling, this page is complete. Just a quick glance at the photo and the simple title and the viewer knows what is taking place. Michelle chose not to include any details about the photo, such as who the child is, because it will be placed in an album, and the album will contain pages that will bring context to the photo.

Supplies: Cardstock; patterned paper (Daisy D's, Jenni Bowlin, My Mind's Eye); rub-ons (7gypsies, Making Memories); journaling card (Jenni Bowlin); flower (Mermaid Tears); chipboard (CherryArte); decorative tape (7gypsies); Misc: adhesive, paint, thread

Erin created this page for an online challenge that asked the question, "What is important to you?" Don't be afraid to use your scrapbook supplies for artistic expression, as Erin did here, rather than memory keeping. Since your scrapbook supplies are familiar to you, they're a great place to start as you work toward artistic freedom.

Supplies: Patterned paper (Around the Block, Creative Imaginations, My Mind's Eye); mask (Heidi Swapp); transparency (My Mind's Eye); brads (Creative·Imaginations, K&Co.); Misc: adhesive, lace, paint, pen

Artwork by Erin Derkatz

My mother-in-law's garden is amazing and something that I preserve with photos every year. When I use them in annual layouts, I don't include journaling because it would be repetitive to write almost the exact message every year. To preserve the memory, I simply include a title that borders the photos and the year.

Supplies: Cardstock; patterned paper, ribbon (SEI); chipboard letters (Zsiage); rub-ons (CherryArte, SEI); Misc: adhesive, thread

DON'T judge A BOOK by its COVER

it is hard when you are a visual person to not judge things by how they look but i am trying & it is paying off!

also something to remember when choosing a book to read, a sandwich or a new CD

CLOTHES are to us what fur and feathers are to beasts and birds; they not only add to our appearance, but they *are* our appearance. How we look to others entirely depends upon what we wear and how we wear it; manners and speech are noted afterward, and character last of all.   Emily Post, 1922

As soon as I saw this patterned paper with a vintage drawing I knew I wanted to create this page as a message to myself. Try finding a themed scrapbook product that gives your story a visual image when your story has no photos. Provide the details of the story in the title and journaling.

Supplies: Cardstock; patterned paper (My Mind's Eye, Paper Salon, Sassafras Lass, Scrapbour); chipboard letters (CherryArte, Heidi Swapp); die-cut shapes (My Mind's Eye); doilies, label (Dollarstore); stamp (Class Act); claim check, clock accent (Papier Valise); Misc: adhesive, ink, staples

YOUR CHALLENGE

Create a page using only scrapbook products to tell a story.

2 RULE

A two-page scrapbook layout should have a left-to-right orientation

A left-to-right page orientation is the standard. It feels natural; we read from left to right and every magazine and book you look at uses this orientation. So what happens when you turn your pages on their sides to create a top-to-bottom orientation? Do your scrapbook pages become incomprehensible? Nothing quite that dramatic occurs. In fact, your pages are given a fresh look that can be used with any subject matter. By breaking this unspoken rule you not only breathe new life into a layout, you are challenged to find new ways of arranging items on your page.

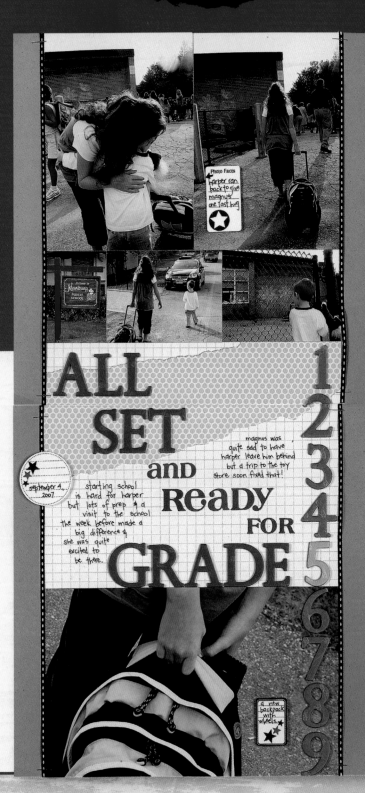

This layout includes everything a typical scrapbook page would, but with just a flip, the page layout gets a unique look. To make the vertical transition easier, start by arranging elements in a two-page scrapbook layout as you normally would—left to right—and then change the page orientation, making slight adjustments in the arrangement as needed.

Supplies: Cardstock; patterned paper (Scenic Route); chipboard letters (Crate Paper); letter stickers (BasicGrey); ribbon (May Arts); tag (CherryArte); Misc: adhesive, pen

YOUR CHALLENGE

Find a two-page layout in your album and re-create it with a vertical orientation.

YOUR CHALLENGE

Create a layout with embellishments and journaling that run down the page.

On this layout, the vertical page orientation enhances the visual movement around the page. Here, the movement is created by the oversized title, the journaling that runs down the page, and the photo at the bottom that anchors the design. When working on your scrapbook page spreads, utilize the page orientation to help make your design flow.

Supplies: Cardstock, patterned paper (Paper Company); chipboard letters (Prima); chipboard accents (Crate Paper); line template (Crafter's Workshop); Misc: adhesive, floss, ink, paint, pen

Here, Ronee has stepped out of her comfort zone to turn her layout on its side. One simple change and this page about an everyday object stands out from other pages in Ronee's album. The rule-breaking treatment automatically creates interest. This technique is suitable for any subject matter, making it a handy creative tool for any page.

Supplies: Image editing software (Adobe); digital butterfly, glitter, letters, patterned paper, stickers by Sausan Designs (Scrapbook Graphics); staple by Vicki Stegall (Oscraps); Misc: stitched letter

Artwork by Ronee Parsons

YOUR CHALLENGE

Create a page about an everyday topic using a vertical orientation.

Breaking
the Rules

ENJOYING
NATURE
07·12·07

YOUR CHALLENGE
Create a lively layout with a top-to-bottom orientation.

Supplies: Cardstock; chipboard letters (Heidi Grace, Zsiage); stamp (artist's own design); Misc: adhesive, ink, pen

The elements are the same for both the layout that follows the rules (on the next page) and this layout that breaks the rules. But one small shift and they look quite different from one another. The layout that follows the rules features a solid design, but the layout that breaks the rules has liveliness and a sense of movement not present in the first. Sometimes just a small, simple change can make a huge difference on your page.

Following the Rules

ENJOYING
NATURE

✓ # Create a Foam Stamp

You will need: Craft foam, adhesive sheet, leaf (or other object to trace), pen, scissors or craft knife, repositionable adhesive, clear stamp block

1

Adhere two pieces of craft foam together using an adhesive sheet.

2

Trace the leaf onto the foam using a pen. Then cut out the design with the craft knife or scissors.

3

Using repositionable adhesive, adhere the stamp to a clear stamping block.

Scrapbook pages should always start with photos

You have tons of pictures to record. And more often than not, they are the catalyst for creating a page. But what if a story inspires a layout? And what if that story doesn't have a photo to go with it? Stories—like fleeting moments and quirky quotes—are important to record. So don't get bound by this rule; important topics, big or small, shouldn't go unscrapped because of a lack of photos. The key to successfully scrapping stories without a starting photo is using general images like simple portraits or pictures of objects. The choice is yours. Just get ready to tell your story first.

Anilu wanted to record this special story—not because of the photos she had but because of the event's significance. And even though photos weren't the start of the page, the general pictures (of sugar skulls) that Anilu took to use on the page create a meaningful tribute to an important event.

Supplies: Cardstock; patterned paper (Jenni Bowlin); stamp (Village Impressions); transparency (Hambly); Misc: adhesive, ink, library card, Mexican bingo cards, pen, staples

Artwork by Anilu Magloire

YOUR CHALLENGE
Create a page about a story and photograph objects to accompany it.

'can you stop my time?'

You get an hour of computer time every day & you never want to waste a second of it. If you need to stop for any reason you can be heard shouting this across the house.

10 years old

When I hear this question from my daughter, I don't think about grabbing my camera. Even if I did, there is no real image that could accurately capture this moment. For this type of layout, a portrait of my daughter works well coupled with a supporting photo of a keyboard.

Supplies: Cardstock; patterned paper (Upsy Daisy); letter stickers (American Crafts); paper bird (Prima); tag (Every Jot & Tittle); Misc: adhesive, floss, pen

YOUR CHALLENGE

Create a page about a daily occurance using two non-specific photos.

→

YOUR CHALLENGE
Create a page about a family member
and use a portrait photo of that person.

Magnus Kade—

age three

OR please & thanks as we say! You are a well mannered little boy even if you don't have the pronunciation down quite yet.

&

Summer 2007

Small children often have adorable ways of saying things, and my son is no exception. I want to remember the way my son speaks before it changes. But his speech patterns are intangible things leaving me without any photo to support the stories. So I matched this story with a simple portrait to create a meaningful page.

Supplies: Cardstock; patterned paper (Heidi Grace, My Mind's Eye); clear arrow (Pageframe); epoxy stickers (SEI); label stickers (Li'l Davis); plastic letters (for tracing) (Maya Road); rub-ons, sticker accent (American Crafts); transparency frame (My Mind's Eye); transparency (Hambly); Misc: adhesive, flock, ink, pen, staples

✓ Create Flocked Letters

You will need: Cardstock, adhesive sheet, loose flock, piece of scrap paper, chipboard or acrylic letters, scissors or craft knife, pencil

Remove one backing from the adhesive sheet. Place your sheet of cardstock on the adhesive sheet. Remove the second backing.

Generously sprinkle flock over the exposed adhesive.

Lay the backing from the adhesive sheet over the flocked area and rub to help adhere the flock. Shake off excess flock and return it to the container.

On the back side of the flocked cardstock, trace the letters in reverse. Cut out the letters using scissors or a craft knife.

RULE 4

Everything on a scrapbook page needs to be straight and perfect

Somewhere along the way you picked up the idea that straight, parallel lines equal the right way to scrapbook. You scrap with your trusty ruler close at hand. After all, straight means perfect and perfect, equals a good page, right? Wrong! It's time to put your rulers away. Creating without this tool allows you more freedom to let your creativity take you where it wants to go. But don't panic.

Try tilting just one photo to start. Then work your way up to an entirely tilted page. You really can think outside the box and create beautiful, successful pages.

If the idea of breaking this rule makes you cringe, then this design is the place to start. On this layout, all the elements are on an angle, but on the same angle, allowing for a bit of order on the page. To re-create this look, start by placing your focal point photo on an angle, and then place all the remaining pieces around the photo on the same angle.

Supplies: Cardstock; patterned paper (Chatterbox, My Mind's Eye); chipboard letters (American Crafts); letter stickers (SEI); transparent letters, flower (Heidi Swapp); chipboard circle (Jenni Bowlin); label stickers (Martha Stewart); rub-ons (Hambly); Misc: adhesive, pen

Artwork by Jeniece Tackett

YOUR CHALLENGE

Create a layout with all the page elements placed on the same angle.

22

good times

i could barely drag the two of you out of the pool — you were having such a great time. this is what summer vacation is all about!

summer '06

This layout is full of subtle contrast: Some items are placed on an angle and some are parallel to the page edges. Placing the supporting photos on angles leads the eye to the solidly placed focal point photo. I gave the same treatment to the title and journaling, creating repetition and unifying the page. Notice that the background pattern is linear. Try using a more free-flowing pattern for a different look.

Supplies: Patterned paper (Creative Imaginations); chipboard letters (K&Co.); Misc: adhesive, pen, staples

YOUR CHALLENGE

Create a page with the journaling and focal point photo placed parallel to the page's edges. Then add supporting photos and a title placed on angles.

rub a dub dub

it's magnus in the tub!

m

...feb 26, 2006...

Clearly adorable in your froggy towel.
Fresh from a bath, all sweet smelling.
Ready for a cuddle, then off to bed.

MADE FOR YOU WITH LOVE

...love those wrinkly toes...

Make a bold statement by placing everything on your page at different angles. On this layout, nearly every embellishment, photo and piece of text is tilted. These simple, varying angles give the page a playful nature, highlighting the layout's theme. To re-create a page like this, place the photos first and then position additional items at angles different from those of the photos.

YOUR CHALLENGE

Create a layout with all the elements at different angles.

Supplies: Cardstock; chipboard letters, clip, snaps (Making Memories); chipboard shapes, clear tag (Heidi Swapp); epoxy shape (KI Memories); ribbon (Michaels, Offray, Wrights); rub-ons (American Crafts, American Traditional); stamp (Technique Tuesday); Misc: adhesive, buttons, labels, paint, pen, staples, thread, wooden sticks

Following the Rules

Supplies: Patterned paper (SEI); die-cut letters (My Mind's Eye); felt arrow, letter stickers (American Crafts); button (Dollarstore); flowers (Blueye Dezines); Misc: adhesive, floss, pen

While the page that follows the rules is nice, it lacks what the page that breaks the rules has—a sense of freedom and fun that is innate to the story. The self-portraits are not framed properly anyway, so angling them makes the imperfection look intentional. Notice that the background design is linear, providing a structured base for the page. This is a great way to combine angles with the perpendicular lines you love.

YOUR CHALLENGE

Create a page with a linear background and elements at various angles.

Breaking the Rules

All elements need to be contained within the page edges

You learned it in kindergarten. And now the idea of staying within the lines has seeped into your creative process. When you see the straight edges of your scrapbook paper it's easy to perceive them as boundaries. But they are artificial borders. Guess what? It's OK to cross the line. The edges of a piece of paper are yours to go beyond. Once you begin to explore outside the boundaries, you will be surprised at the instant energy that radiates from your pages.

A visit to the Dr.'s office after she turned one year old revealed that Mia was small for her age. At the time she weighed 16 lbs. when the average was 21 lbs. Needless to say I was very worried. What happened? What did I do wrong? We've been going to back for weight check-ups every month since then and I've been feeding her as much as she will eat. In spite of her small size, Mia is very happy, full of energy, and is so smart. I think she's doing really well right now.

little one

Oversized elements can often overwhelm a page. But here Michelle has balanced the large flower by extending it off the page. Giving the flower a precarious placement off the edge places less importance on it. The flower keeps from becoming overpowering while still serving as the symbol of contrast that Michelle wanted to mark against the small size of her daughter.

Supplies: Cardstock; patterned paper (Daisy D's, Prima); label (Making Memories); flower stamens (Impress); flowers (Prima); paper trim (Doodlebug); stamps (Hero Arts, October Afternoon); brads (American Crafts, Prima); Misc: adhesive, ink

Artwork by Michelle Guray

YOUR CHALLENGE

Create a page with an oversized element that extends off an edge of the page.

YOUR CHALLENGE

Create a page with one or two minor elements extending off the edges.

When adding elements that go beyond the page border, a little can go a long way. Here, I extended photos just past the edges and let my embellishment burst off the top. It's just enough to give this New Year's page pizzazz. If you're concerned about fitting pages like this inside an album, reduce the size of your pages (as I did here) to account for the off-the-page elements.

Supplies: Transparency (Hambly); chipboard shapes (Everlasting Keepsakes); embossing glitter, stamps (Gel-a-tins); felt and plastic shapes (American Crafts); ribbon (Die Cuts with a View, Offray); Misc: adhesive, buttons, coaster, ink, pen

For extra interest, I cut the right side of this page into a wavy border and embellished it with floral accents. I planned to keep the page small enough to fit into a page protector, but during its creation, it grew larger than I intended. Instead of dwelling on this roadblock, I set it aside and let creativity guide me.

Supplies: Patterned paper (BasicGrey); transparency (Hambly); chipboard letters (Creative Imaginations); chipboard shapes (Everlasting Keepsakes); flowers (Blueye Dezines);z mask (Heidi Swapp); ribbon (Wrights); rub-ons (KI Memories); tag (Every Jot & Tittle); Misc: adhesive, floss, gems, paint, pen, staples

↙

YOUR CHALLENGE

Alter the edge of a page before adding elements that extend beyond it.

chapter

2

two dear soles

{a tribute}

for all the
running,
jumping,
pounding,
skipping,
sprinting
you put up
with

for all the
sweat
you endure

for all the
terrain and
miles
you have
travelled

MY BUTT
sincerely
THANKS YOU

he's been issued his packing slip.

at age 3 magnus no longer depends on Peggy.

SUBJECT DOES MATTER:
Page Topics That Rule Our Scrapbooks

Scrapbookers have different reasons for scrapbooking. But the majority will say they scrapbook to preserve their lives. For most, this means following the same sequence: The camera comes out at an event, photos are snapped and then the photos along with a written story are used to create a scrapbook page. By following this pattern you end up recording only a percentage of your real life. Think about it. How much of your life involves birthdays and family vacations? Not much, I suspect. You are a dimensional person with an interesting, full and complicated life, obsessions and interests, and your scrapbooks should reflect this. To truly capture your real life—your real family and the real you—you need to include several aspects of your life into your scrapbooks. It's time to break from the traditional ideas of the "right" page topics and start capturing the big with the little.

RULE 6

All scrapbook pages need to have deep meaning

Your life is not serious all the time (I hope!), so why do all of your scrapbook pages reflect heavy themes? While I agree that significant topics with deep meaning should be included in your scrapbooks, there is no reason albums need to be exclusive. By looking at aspects of your life with a little humor or light-hearted musing, you get a new perspective on daily life. More often than not you will find these types of pages end up revealing yourself in a way that is unexpected, yet truly you.

A serious page just wouldn't be appropriate when writing about a kitchen tool. Anilu's layout provides a humorous perspective that perfectly evokes the affection she has for her mixer. Pages like Anilu's provide a great way to see how your affections, or your family's, change over time.

Supplies: Patterned paper (Collage Press, KI Memories); letter stickers (American Crafts); ribbon (Making Memories); Misc: adhesive, pen

YOUR CHALLENGE

Create a scrapbook page showing your affection for an object in a lighthearted way.

she's the one

She fills our home with sweet treats. She lets me experiment with her. She gives me all the bragging right. She makes us all so happy!! 8/07

Artwork by Anilu Magloire

YOUR CHALLENGE

Scrap a very common or slightly embarrassing aspect of yourself.

The humorous perspective this page is written from captures both my lousy housekeeping skills and my sense of humor. It really expresses the real me, so it's a great way to connect with the viewer. We all have stuff like this in our lives, things we may find slightly embarrassing, but they lend color and character to our albums.

Supplies: Patterned paper (Scrapbour); transparency (Hambly); chipboard letters (Creative Imaginations); buttons, sticker accents (SEI); journaling tag (Heidi Swapp); stamps (Making Memories); flowers (EK Success); rhinestones, sequins (Westrim); rub-ons (Autumn Leaves, Scrapworks, Stemma); tags (Prima); Misc: adhesive, floss, paint, pen

With a clever title and tongue-in-cheek journaling, Erin has created a humorous tribute to an object that most days never gets a second thought. From this page, you learn about Erin, her running habit and her sense of humor, and she comes across as a three-dimensional person. A page like this captures the viewer's attention and lets your real voice come through.

YOUR CHALLENGE

Create a lighthearted page about a personal habit.

Supplies: Cardstock; patterned paper (Fancy Pants, Scenic Route); rub-ons (Autumn Leaves, Heidi Swapp); mulberry paper (PSX); Misc: adhesive, gold floral accent, paint, pen

Artwork by Erin Derkatz

RULE 7

Scrapbook pages should show only the big events in life

What do you see when you flip through your albums? Your son's birthday? Last Christmas? A trip to the beach? Of course you want to relive these special days. But those are hard to forget; they're clearly marked on the calendar. Life is made up of a lot of little moments and if left out of your scrapbooks, your real life is not fully recorded. Sometimes breaking a rule is not only creative but necessary. If you made an album that included only big events, your album would house just a skeleton of your life. The little stuff is what rounds out a scrapbook (and your life) and makes it complete.

fading memories

it is true what bad memories fade with time. it is hard to believe that just over a year ago you had lung surgery that removed 2/3 of your lung. at the time i felt we would never forget the terror of it but time has moved on & all that is left is a distant memory & a faded scar.

Although this page is related to a significant event, the layout itself is about how my perspective on the event has changed. I have pages documenting my son's surgery, but I wanted a layout that reflects how I now feel about that time. Pages with new perspectives show how feelings change with time and offer a way to continue your story.

Supplies: Patterned paper (American Crafts, Heidi Grace); chipboard letters (K&Co.); clear letters (Heidi Swapp); felt shapes (American Crafts, Dollarstore); foam arrow (American Crafts); Misc: adhesive, paint, pen

YOUR CHALLENGE
Create a page about how you now feel about a past event.

YOUR CHALLENGE
Create a page about a
child's mini milestone.

he's
been
issued
his
packing
slip.

no longer depends on froggy.

at age 3 magnus

We often record major milestones
in our children's lives, but the little
ones sometimes get overlooked.
Years from now, I will probably
remember my son's favorite stuffed
animal and how he became
attached to it. But I probably
won't remember when he moved
past this little bit of babyhood.
A quick and simple page, like this
6" × 12" (15cm × 30cm) layout,
is all that is needed to record and
treasure a small event like this.

*Supplies: Cork sheet (Karen Foster); letter stickers
(American Crafts); Misc: adhesive, pen, staples*

33

Artwork by Janine Langer

Even grumpy faces can be adorable, as seen in Janine's photos. A small, insignificant event triggered her son's grumpy face, but Janine thought the moment important enough to capture. Positive and negative mood changes both make for great real-life pages. Be sure to remain sensitive to your subject's feelings if anything negative is recorded.

Supplies: Cardstock; patterned paper (Cosmo Cricket, Creative Imaginations); chipboard letters (American Crafts); stamp, sticker, tag (7gypsies); brad (Bazzill); label by Jennifer Pebbles (Two Peas in a Bucket); Misc: adhesive, ink

Journaling Translation
You are so cute when you are annoyed sometimes. Especially when I like to take a picture of the moment, like a superstar.

YOUR CHALLENGE
Scrap about a mood change in yourself or someone else.

Artwork by Jeniece Tackett

This page perfectly captures something that is indeed very small: a simple thing said in passing by Jeniece's daughter. Most young children mispronounce things in adorable ways. At the time they are often repeated, but if they are not recorded, they will soon be forgotten. Take time to record these little moments before they are erased from your memory.

Supplies: Patterned paper (BasicGrey, Daisy D's); chipboard letters (Heidi Swapp, Li'l Davis); letter stickers, plastic letters (Heidi Swapp); die-cut shapes (Daisy D's, My Mind's Eye); flower (American Crafts); label stickers (Jenni Bowlin, Papier Valise); rickrack, rub-ons (Making Memories); ribbon (Michaels); brads (Imaginisce, Making Memories); stamps (Karen Foster); Misc: adhesive, ink, pen

YOUR CHALLENGE

Record a quirky quotation or a funny mispronunciation on a scrapbook page.

That's right, don't get mad, get scrapping! Scrapbook those crazy moments in life that make you want to scream and laugh, all at the same time. If you can remember in the moment to grab your camera, these small, everyday mishaps make for great family pages.

YOUR CHALLENGE
Create a page about a mishap.

Supplies: Patterned paper, sticker trim (My Mind's Eye); chipboard letters (Crate Paper); chipboard shapes (Bo-Bunny, Everlasting Keepsakes); Misc: adhesive, paint, pen

The subject of a scrapbook page should always be a person or pet

You didn't sign a contract giving your loved ones, with two feet or four, exclusive rights to your pages. Of course you want to scrap your friends and family. But it's OK to capture the other things too—objects that are as much a part of your life as the people who surround you. Nobody is going to begrudge you a little space in your albums for topics outside the norm. Your favorite obsession? A crazy sign? Feel free to scrap a page! In fact, people will appreciate getting to see you as a real person through tributes to what makes your life whole. And by tearing down this rule you open yourself up to an unlimited number of page topics and allow a fresh perspective on who you are.

This kind of page doesn't require a lot of time or thought; it's a chance to play. Next time you see something that catches your eye, no matter the reason, photograph it and then include it on a scrapbook page. Use this type of page as a way to really let loose and foster your creativity.

Supplies: Patterned paper (Crate Paper); chipboard letters (Heidi Swapp); fabric stickers (Making Memories); transparency (Hambly); stamps (Purple Onion); chipboard arrows (Everlasting Keepsakes); tag (Every Jot & Tittle); Misc: adhesive, embossing powder, ink, pen, rhinestones, staples

YOUR CHALLENGE
Photograph a sign that catches your eye and create a page about it.

Favorite possessions, like this much-loved gadget of mine, are part of everyone's life, but stories or thoughts about them are usually absent from our albums. Favorite items often change over time so it's important to document them. This will provide a glimpse of the person behind the object and how his or her tastes change over time.

Supplies: Cardstock; patterned paper (Paper Company); chipboard letters (Zsiage); letter stickers (Arctic Frog); doodling template (Crafter's Workshop); vintage metalheads (Papier Valise); Misc: adhesive, felt, gems, pen

If you have a collection, create a page about it. You can choose an individual piece to showcase, like Ronee has here, or the entire collection. Make sure to record the story behind the piece or collection. Including these treasures on a page is a great way to record the collection's history if it will be handed down to future generations.

Supplies: Image editing software (Adobe); digital patterned papers by Dana Frantz and Sausan Designs (Scrapbook Graphics); label, letters, staples by Vicki Stegall (Oscraps); paper tear by Steph Krush (Digital Paper Tearing)

Artwork by Ronee Parsons

YOUR CHALLENGE
Photograph a collection and document it on a scrapbook page.

RULE 9

Always use a self-portrait to feature yourself on a page

You can admit it, as soon as you read *self-portrait* you were ready to move past this one. Let me guess: You hate to have your picture taken. Or perhaps you're always the one behind the camera. Either way, when looking through photos, you are never pictured. No more excuses! Now is the time to find clever ways to include yourself in your albums. After all, most of your scrapbook pages will be written from your perspective and readers will want to know the person behind it all.

One way to include yourself in your albums is to create a page about your favorites, like your favorite foods or music or a favorite physical feature or personality trait. On this page, I documented my favorite physical feature by photographing just the feature and journaling a bit about it. If you're not sure what you should include, ask a friend or family member.

Supplies: Cardstock; clear letters (Maya Road); date sticker (7gypsies); butterfly (Dollarstore); label sticker (Martha Stewart); library card (Papier Valise); rub-ons (7gypsies, Hambly); sticker trim (My Mind's Eye); Misc: adhesive, pen

GOOD HAIR DAYS

so happy that my hair is long again.

it pretty much guarantees good hair days.

DATE: 08/07/07

YOUR CHALLENGE
Create a page about your favorite physical feature or personality trait, looking for interesting ways to photograph it.

Artwork by Erin Derkatz

Another way to include yourself on a page is to gather photos that carry a particular theme from different periods in your life, as Erin has done. For your own page, gather photos of places you visit in your hometown or photos from a favorite view during different seasons. Provide a brief explanation of how they represent you and you have a great page—no self-portrait required.

Supplies: Cardstock; patterned paper (Melissa Frances); stamps (7gypsies, Fancy Pants, Making Memories, Stampabilities); rub-on (Making Memories); tab (Cosmo Cricket); Misc: adhesive, ink, pen

Habits make for great page topics by offering a quick look into your life without exposing you too much. Use photos with you in them, as I've done here, or find ways to photograph your habit without being in the photo. Stumped for ideas? People close to you will easily be able to list habits that are distinctly you (loveable or annoying!).

Supplies: Patterned paper, transparency frame (My Mind's Eye); letter stickers (American Crafts); ribbon (Fancy Pants); stamp (Gel-a-tins); Misc: adhesive, felt, paint, pen, staples

39

Artwork by Michelle Guray

YOUR CHALLENGE

Create a page that represents your life using photos of things that surround you.

This layout is a clever example of a way to include yourself on a scrapbook page. Michelle has created a photo collage of meaningful items that surround her every day. When creating a page that records who you are, you can include objects that surround you, items you are thinking about or even the scene outside your window. Record what the images mean to you or how they connect to you.

Supplies: Cardstock; stickers (7gypsies, ARTchix); photo corners (American Crafts); quote by Jackie Eckles (Designer Digitals); Misc: adhesive, pen

This page captures a small detail about me that is unknown to most people. Even though my face is not seen, it's clear this page is about me, and it offers a glimpse into my life that otherwise would not be revealed. These types of pages are great for avoiding the dreaded self-portrait while speaking very clearly about yourself.

YOUR CHALLENGE

Create a page about something that most people don't know about you.

Supplies: Cardstock; patterned paper, rub-ons, transparency (Hambly); crochet flower (artist's own design); chipboard shape (Everlasting Keepsakes); paper trim (Doodlebug); stamp (Zingboom); Misc: adhesive, envelope, felt, floss, paint, pen, staples

Make Fast Freehand Felt Letters
You will need: Felt, scissors

1 Cut rectangles from felt in the approximate size of the letters you want to make.

2 Cut a letter from each rectangle freehand. Start by cutting the straight parts of the letter. Cut any round parts next.

3 To cut the inner circle of a letter, make a small cut with the scissors. Then slowly cut a small circle, gradually making it bigger until you have the size you want.

chapter 3

SOLID

married for four years & we had our fair share of ups & downs but through it all we have remained solid. I cannot imagine one moment of life without you.

august 2007

you received incredible care while at sick kids & nurse wooby was a favourite. every time she came to check on you she would practice 'fishy' faces with you until you finally got it. this simple act of care made a huge impact on you (heart) you change nurse wooby.

NURSE "WOO BY"

a.k.a. nurse ruby

15 APR 2006

THE GOOD, THE BAD AND THE UGLY:
The Rules That Govern Our Photos

Photos set the stage for the stories we want to tell and provide illustrations of the memories we want to share. As with any other aspect of scrapbooking, numerous rules apply to photos to help us "improve" our pages. Photo rules generally fall into two categories: the types of photos to use and how to use them on a page. Part of breaking the rules and achieving creative freedom is deciding for yourself which photos are worth keeping and the best way to use them. You need to throw out the "dos and don'ts" of using photos so you can trust your instincts and create pages that best capture your memories. As they say, beauty is in the eye of the beholder.

10 RULE

Only good photos should be used on your scrapbook pages

If you're like me, you take a lot of photos. Some turn out wonderfully, and others, well, not so good. As a photographer, you want to use the photos that are in focus, well composed and well lit; as a scrapbooker you want to record every memory. At times, it's hard to reconcile the two. Sometimes, the only photos you have of a moment are less than stellar. You can choose to exclude them because you don't want anyone to see them. Or you can choose to showcase them anyway and allow them to enhance your page as they can—and will. You might be surprised by what the not-so-nice photos add to a story.

It's sometimes hard to capture a child's genuine smile, so as soon as Anilu saw this photo she knew she had to scrap it. Unfortunately, the photo was off-center. Instead of cropping it, Anilu decided to work with what she had and played up the look of the photo. Placing the photo on the edge of the page makes the imperfect framing look intentional.

Supplies: Cardstock; patterned paper (BasicGrey); labels (Autumn Leaves, Jenni Bowlin); die-cut shape (QuicKutz); pin (Heidi Grace); Misc: adhesive, felt, ink, lace, stamps

YOUR CHALLENGE
Enhance an off-center photo by placing it creatively on a page.

Artwork by Anilu Magloire

2007

a smile
that melts
my heart

44

Artwork by Erin Derkatz

Some scrappers might not have used a photo like this because it's out of focus and the subject's head is cut off. But Erin felt differently. The photo captures her daughter in a way that a perfectly posed and focused photo could not. The look expresses the feeling that her daughter's excitement was so great no photo frame could contain it. And the blur creates a sense of movement and gives the page energy.

Supplies: Cardstock; patterned paper (KI Memories); stamps (Fancy Pants, Making Memories); chipboard heart (BasicGrey); transparency frame (My Mind's Eye); Misc: adhesive, embossing pen and powder, floss, lace, paint, pen, staples

YOUR CHALLENGE
Scrap a photo that evokes a feeling of movement because of a blurry subject.

you received incredible care while at sick kids & nurse wooby was a favourite. every time she came to check on you she would practice 'fishy faces' with you until you finally got it. this simple act of care made a huge impact on us. thank you nurse wooby.

NURSE "WOO BY"

a.k.a. nurse ruby

1 5 APR 2006

During a very trying period in my family's life, a special nurse came along to give us a bit of sunshine. Due to high stress at the time, I did not think to photograph her, but I did photograph my son making the faces she taught him to make. The photos were poorly lit and out of focus, but they were all I had from those special moments. To help improve the photos, I converted them to black and white.

YOUR CHALLENGE
Convert imperfect photos to black and white and use them on a scrapbook page.

Supplies: Patterned paper (Crate Paper, Melissa Frances, Prima); chipboard letters (Crate Paper); rub-on letters (American Crafts); date stamp (Dollarstore); die-cut frame (Prima); ribbon (Stemma); vintage label (Papier Valise); Misc: adhesive, graph paper, pen, photo corners

Magnus

the first present you opened on your birthday contained a bag of m&m's. the look on your face was completely priceless when you realized they were all for you. april '07

m&m's

3rd birthday

Supplies: Cardstock; chipboard letters (Scenic Route, Zsiage); ribbon (Strano); Misc: adhesive, paint, pen, staples

An error with the camera setting resulted in some out-of-focus photos from my son's birthday. It was disappointing at first, but this was an important event to scrap. I had two options for creating a page: I could take a new photo, which you can see on the layout that follows the rules. Or I could use the out-of-focus photos that captured my son's expressions, as seen on the layout that breaks the rules. Both pages tell the same story, but the layout with the "bad" photos transports the viewer into the moment.

Breaking the Rules

Supplies: Letter stickers, patterned paper, rub-ons, sticker accents (American Crafts); photo corners (Heidi Swapp); Misc: adhesive, pen

april 2007

3rd birthday

first present opened

pure BLISS

your face was completely priceless when you discovered the bag of m&m's in your birthday package.

YOUR CHALLENGE

Use photos with bad lighting or blurry subjects from a memorable event on a scrapbook page.

11 RULE

Photos should be cropped tightly around the subject

When taking photos, you probably try to fill your camera frame with your subject. Or afterward, you crop your photos so the subject is front and center. After all, close-up photos capture detail, and a centered subject provides balance. But detail and symmetry don't always make for the best photos. Photos cropped tightly around a subject can lose their context, and can make for boring pages. Using creative framing in a photo, whether your subject is off to one side or in the distance, provides perspective, plus a little drama for a layout.

  With digital photography, this rule is a fairly simple one to break. Take a photo from far away and then you can play around and use it as you like. Keep the photo wide for an interesting perspective; crop it off-center for a creative shot.

This page is a great example of how empty space in a photo serves a purpose on a layout. Here, the dark areas created by keeping the subject off-center help draw the eye to my son's hands and face. And because I converted the photo to black and white, the dark space provides a wonderful contrast to his pale skin.

Supplies: Cardstock; patterned paper (Crate Paper, Scenic Route); chipboard letters and heart (Heidi Grace); rub-ons (CherryArte); stamp (Purple Onion); tag (Every Jot & Tittle); Misc: adhesive, ink, paint, pen, photo corners

YOUR CHALLENGE
Photograph (or crop) your subject in the left or right third of the frame and use the photo on a page.

WHEN DID YOU

Once upon a time...

Es kommt mir vor als warst Du erst gestern zur Welt gekommen. Die Zeit vergeht so schnell. Du wirst immer größer und selbständiger. Gib mir bitte noch etwas Zeit, mich daran zu gewöhnen!

08.07

remember when not so long ago

don't forget when you were a baby remember that time?

GROW UP SO

FAST

When cropping the large photo on this layout, Janine cut closely and purposefully off-center around her son's face, making an interesting frame. Creatively framing your subject with your camera is not always possible in the moment, but the beauty of digital photography is that you can crop it after the fact, opening up artistic possibilities for nearly any photo.

Supplies: Cardstock; patterned paper (My Mind's Eye, Sassafras Lass); chipboard letters, clock accent, letter stickers (Heidi Swapp); journal card, sticker accents (My Mind's Eye); transparency (Hambly); word stickers (Making Memories); brad, stamp (7gypsies); Misc: adhesive, ink, pen

Artwork by Janine Langer

YOUR CHALLENGE
Crop a photo to create off-center framing around the subject.

Journaling Translation
It often feels as if you were born only yesterday. Time goes on so fast, you are getting older and more and more independent each day. Please give me some more time to become accustomed to it.

But whatever road you choose,
I'm right behind you,
Win or lose
—Rod Stewart

Artwork by Michelle Guray

*Aidan,
I'm behind you all the way.
xoxo.
Mommy*

Supplies: Cardstock; patterned paper (7gypsies, Autumn Leaves, My Mind's Eye); chipboard accents (CherryArte, Junkitz); die-cut transparency (My Mind's Eye); digital brush by Rhonna Farrer (Two Peas in a Bucket); tag (Jenni Bowlin); measuring tape (7gypsies); rhinestones (Doodlebug); Misc: adhesive

Michelle's picture is not the standard close-up photo scrapbookers often favor. This one shows her son in silhouette, cycling off into the distance with most of the photo showing the background. Michelle could have easily cropped out all of the "extra" background. Instead, she kept it to lend the photo a sense of atmosphere and context, which adds to the message of her page.

YOUR CHALLENGE

Photograph your subject from a distance, and use the whole photo on a layout.

Following the Rules

Comparing these two layouts makes it easy to see the positive difference that leaving a photo un-cropped makes. By layering the journaling over the photo on the layout that breaks the rules, I created a connection between the two, making a more unified page. Before deciding if you should crop a photo, look for ways to utilize the space for other elements in your design.

Supplies: Cardstock; patterned paper (CherryArte); chipboard letters (American Crafts); Misc: adhesive

Breaking the Rules

YOUR CHALLENGE
Use the "extra" space in a photo to write your journaling.

12 RULE

You should emphasize a focal point photo through size or color

Changing the size or color of a focal point photo in order to draw attention to it is quick, simple and straight to the point. But what happens when you do not have the space for an enlargement, a color change would take away from the page design or those techniques have simply become monotonous? Time to break the rules and use new ways to emphasize a photo. A bold page element grabs the viewer's attention. Hand-drawn effects or subtle embellishments direct the eye. Matting one photo will let the reader know where to look first. Any of these techniques can be used effectively to create interest around the focus of your layout.

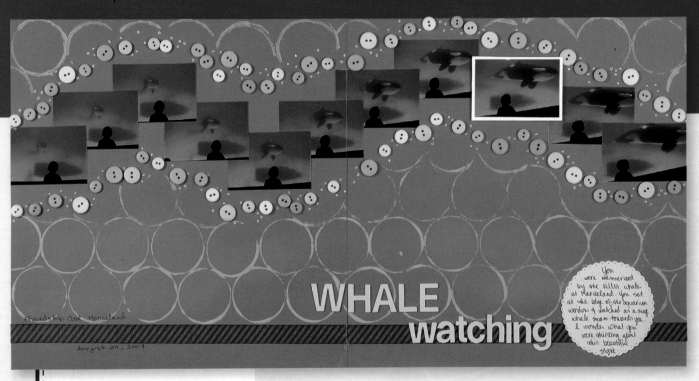

YOUR CHALLENGE
Create a page with simple matting around the focal photo, adding adhesvie foam if desired.

One of the most straightforward ways to emphasize a focal photo is to matte it in a contrasting color. In this series of almost identical photos, this simple treatment, along with the lift given to the photo by adhesive foam, makes it very clear which photo I want to stand out. Remember, sometimes the simplest of methods is the most effective.

Supplies: Cardstock; chipboard letters (Heidi Swapp); buttons (SEI); ribbon (Michaels); stamp (drinking glass); Misc: adhesive, decorative scissors, paint, pen

Although Janine has used the same photo repeatedly, there is still clear emphasis on one in particular. The focal photo has a white border, which creates individuality as well as contrast to the black in the image. Janine surrounded it with a triangle of embellishments, which also draw the eye to the image. Either of these techniques can be used on pages you create, even if the photo is not repeated.

Supplies: Cardstock; patterned paper (American Crafts, Creative Imaginations, Tinkering Ink); chipboard letters (Heidi Swapp); rub-on (BasicGrey); sticker (7gypsies); stamp (Autumn Leaves); butterfly brush by Cherie Mask (Two Peas in a Bucket); Misc: adhesive, buttons, ink, pen, thread

Journaling Translation

30 years old, a great husband, a wonderful son, a beautiful house and a perfect hobby. I love my life.

YOUR CHALLENGE

Create a page with embellishments carefully placed to highlight the focal photo.

Artwork by Jeniece Tackett

YOUR CHALLENGE

Create a page using two techniques that emphasize the focal point photo.

Jeniece uses two separate methods on this page to emphasize the focal point photo of her daughter learning to tie her shoes. The most obvious is the bold arrow that circles the page and points directly to the most important photo. The second method is more subtle than the first: She selected a focal point photo with a vertical orientation while using supporting photos that have a horizontal orientation, making the vertical photo stand out. Both methods are effective whether you use them alone or together on one page.

Supplies: Patterned paper (Daisy D's); chipboard letters (American Crafts); letter stickers, rhinestone circle (Heidi Swapp); stamps (7gypsies, Karen Foster); chipboard button (KI Memories); die-cut shapes (Making Memories, Scenic Route); flower (Bo-Bunny); journaling tags (Daisy D's, Heidi Swapp); label sticker (Martha Stewart); Misc: adhesive, ink, pen

When using a group of similar photos, it can be hard to showcase a focal point photo. But the method shown here makes it easy. I simply placed the focal point photo in the center of the group along with a white border and a thought bubble, making the focal point photo effectively emphasized.

Supplies: Cardstock; patterned paper (BasicGrey, Scenic Route); letter stickers, rub-on letters (American Crafts); journaling sticker (Martha Stewart); Misc: adhesive, pen

YOUR CHALLENGE
Create a page with the focal point photo placed in the center of a group.

Another way to highlight a focal point photo is to offset it from other photos. On this page, the supporting photos are placed in two groups with the images nearly touching. The focal point photo, however, is set apart. This treatment piques a viewer's curiosity, drawing her in to discover why the photo is on its own.

Supplies: Cardstock; patterned paper (Anna Griffin); chipboard letters (Heidi Swapp); arrow sticks, rub-on letters (American Crafts); stamp (CherryArte); Misc: adhesive, ink, pen, staples

YOUR CHALLENGE
Create a page with the focal point photo offset from supporting photos.

13 RULE

When using only one photo, the photo should be enlarged

Typically, we think a large photo makes the biggest impact. But placing one small photo on a page can make just as big a statement as using a large one. The secret is balance, whether your layout is full of elements, or you leave breathing room around the photo. Whatever your style, if you're conscious of maintaining balance, you can successfully use a small, single photo on a page.

This page balances one photo with an expanse of white space. The band of patterned paper is the key to success because it anchors the photo to the page. This page has visual impact because of its simplicity.

Supplies: Software (Adobe); digital patterned paper by Ronee Parsons (Oscraps) and (Shabby Princess); flower petal, overlay, staple by Vicki Stegall (Oscraps); patch (Shabby Princess)

Artwork by Ronee Parsons

YOUR CHALLENGE
Create a page with one small photo and a white background.

Here, clustering embellishments around the photo gives the area visual weight and creates balance against the space on the rest of the page. Converting the photo to black and white also helps the photo stand out.

Supplies: Patterned paper (Crate Paper, Melissa Frances); chipboard letters (Crate Paper); letter stickers (Making Memories); die-cut tags (Daisy D's); rub-ons (Fontwerks); stamp (Anna Griffin); tag (7gypsies); Misc: adhesive, decorative scissors, pen, staples

YOUR CHALLENGE
Reduce a favorite photo to wallet size and frame with a group of embellishments.

SOLID

married for four years & we had our
fair share of ups & downs but through it
all we have remained solid.
i cannot imagine one moment of life without you.

august 2007

When using a standard-sized photo, it's easy to fear it will get lost on the page, especially if you're placing it on top of a busy pattern. But using a solid cardstock mat, like I used here, distinguishes the picture from the background. Plus, the muted photo and solid mat provide a resting place for the eye, drawing it in and letting the photo take center stage.

Supplies: Cardstock; letter stickers, patterned paper (American Crafts); Misc: adhesive foam, decorative scissors, pen

YOUR CHALLENGE
Create a page with a small photo on top of a busy patterned paper.

Create Paper Lace
You will need: 2 sheets of patterned paper, small sharp scissors, a craft knife, adhesive foam

1 Carefully cut around portions of the design on the patterned paper with scissors. Cut any inner edges with a craft knife.

2 On the wrong side of the paper, apply adhesive foam liberally, making sure to support small areas. (Cut foam squares smaller as needed to fit.)

3 Remove the backing from the adhesive foam in a corner of the cut-out paper. Apply this to the background paper, lining up the papers' edges. Remove the remaining backings and adhere the rest of the cut-out paper.

chapter **4**

these girls
make me laugh
...until my sides hurt.

CHA summer '07

michele,
catherine,
katrina
& i

you
&
me

it's funny what it's rare to find a photo of the two of us. you would think with me always having a camera in hand there would be lots but this photo is a year old & there is not a more recent one to be found. this is something i've got to remedy 'cause when we're old i want to see how good we looked, how young & oh so happy!!!

october 2006
photo taken at sunset on the beach. a moment stolen away during thanksgiving in sarnia.

CREATIVE COLORING:
The Rules About Color

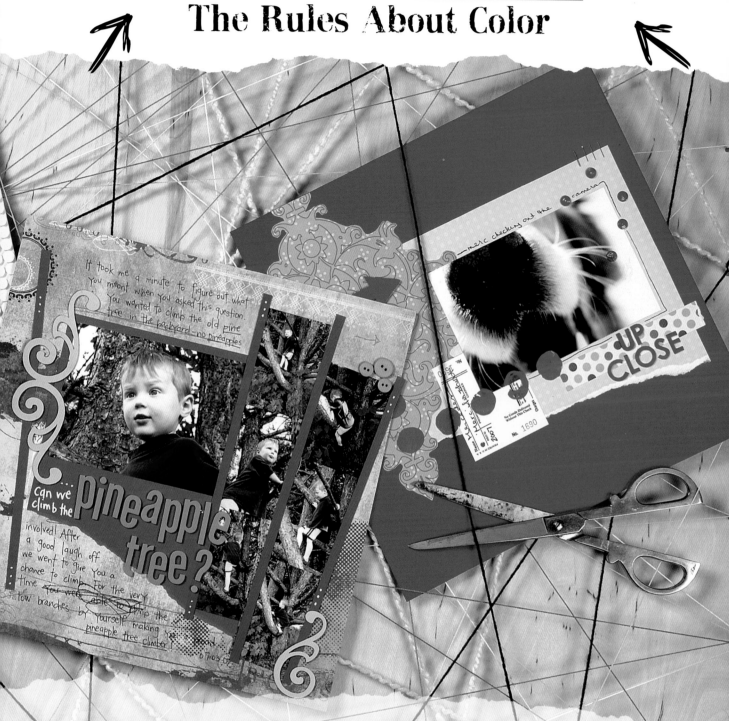

It took me a minute to figure out what you meant when you asked this question. You wanted to climb the old pine tree in the backyard—no pineapples

can we climb the pineapple tree?

involved! After a good laugh off we went to give you a chance to climb. For the very time you were able to climb the low branches by yourself making you the pineapple tree climber.
07/03/05

—merc checking out the camera

UP CLOSE

Color has its own language, and the colors you choose send subtle messages. But because color choices are almost unlimited, choosing them can be overwhelming. So you rely on the rules to tell you what to do. When thinking about colors for your pages, look beyond the safe choices like matching hues and neighbors on the color wheel. These choices limit you, and color choices should be limited only by your imagination. Stretch yourself to use colors in new ways and be on the lookout for unexpected sources of color inspiration. Using color combinations beyond the obvious creates a dramatic page. Perhaps you've been intimidated to try something outside the norm. Here's your permission: If you like a color, go for it!

Scrapbook page colors should come directly from your photos

This rule is tried and true—and completely safe. It's great for beginners who often feel overwhelmed by all the color choices. You, however, are ready for the next step. Chances are you've already broken this rule without realizing it. Take your holiday pages: They're more likely to feature colors that echo the season (like red and green) than colors that match the photos. You can apply this same thought process to other pages to use colors in new ways. Look beyond your photos and try using colors to establish a mood, evoke an emotion or create interest.

The effect of the colors used on this page is subtle. The yellow-orange color mimics the light reflected on the photo's subject. Erin breaks the rules by choosing a color implied in the photo rather than one specifically in it. Including orange on the page enhances the photo, making the summer sun appear to radiate off the page.

Supplies: Cardstock; patterned paper (KI Memories); buttons (Autumn Leaves); chipboard shape (Deluxe Designs); Misc: adhesive, floss, paint, pen, staples

Artwork by Erin Derkatz

YOUR CHALLENGE

Choose colors for your page based on what you want the photo to project.

YOUR CHALLENGE
Create a page using a color that is complementary to the main color in your photo.

she rocks my world

Artwork by Anilu Magloire

The typical choice for this page might have been green, matched to the little girl's dress. Instead, Anilu chose a color scheme of pink and orange. Using complementary colors makes both the pink and the green appear vibrant. And using pink and orange, rather than green, ensures the photo does not blend into the background.

Supplies: Cardstock; patterned paper (American Crafts); flowers (Prima); dress tag, library card (Papier Valise); stamps (Village Impressions); Misc: adhesive, brads, ink

The color of the flowers dominates these photos, making it an obvious choice for a background color. Instead, I chose a color that enhances the photos instead of matching them. On this particular page, I used colors that fall on either side of orange on the color wheel—yellow and red. This helps achieve a sense of harmony on the page. Using a vivid orange in the background might have competed with the photos rather than enhancing them.

Supplies: Cardstock; chipboard letters (Zsiage); letter stickers (Staples); flower sequins (Westrim); stamp (Label Tulip); Misc: adhesive, embossing powder, ink, pen

YOUR CHALLENGE

Create a page using colors that fall on either side of the photo's dominate color on the color wheel.

Following the Rules

these girls

make me laugh...

Supplies: Cardstock; patterned paper (Bo-Bunny, My Mind's Eye); chipboard letters, felt arrow (American Crafts); stamps (Purple Onion); Misc: adhesive, ink, paint, pen

On the layout that follows the rules, I picked the teal in the photo to use as the dominant color in the layout. As you can see, choosing colors from your photo is simple, but it can make for a dull page. To make the photos really pop on the layout that breaks the rules, I used shades of plum and green, which are nowhere in the photos but coordinate with teal. The contrast in colors makes for a vibrant page, one with energy that matches the photos.

Breaking the Rules

these girls

make me laugh...

YOUR CHALLENGE

Pick one dominant color from your photo and choose two coordinating colors to use on a page.

Supplies: Cardstock; patterned paper (Chatterbox, My Mind's Eye, Polar Bear Press); chipboard letters, felt arrow (American Crafts); stamps (Purple Onion); Misc: adhesive, ink, paint, pen

Don't use neutral colors on a page because they look dull

When you read the words "neutral colors," do you picture the dullest beige possible? How boring! Like all colors, neutrals come in a variety of hues. Black, white, cream and gray—and their many shades—all fall into the neutral category. By their very nature, neutrals provide an unobtrusive back-drop for your photos, making the elements on your page really pop. Once you challenge yourself to work with neutrals and find out how versatile they really are, you'll never again see neutrals as dull.

When creating a page in neutrals, you don't have to mask your entire background in brown patterns. Try using a solid cardstock accented with bits of neutral prints. By cutting various brown patterned papers into a uniform size and shape, Anilu was able to achieve variety with little color. Clever use of a gold pen brings a bit of sophisticated shine to this neutral palette.

Supplies: Cardstock; patterned paper (7gypsies, BasicGrey); stamp (PSX); metal embellishment (Anna Griffin); ticket (Jenni Bowlin); Misc: adhesive, gold stars, ink, pen

Artwork by Anilu Magloire

YOUR CHALLENGE

Incorporate small pieces of neutral patterned papers on a page with a solid background.

Artwork by Ronee Parsons

↓

YOUR CHALLENGE

Create a layout using brown patterned paper for the background.

This page is covered in neutral colors, but it's anything but dull. Instead of relying on color to give her page visual interest, Ronee used texture, layers and patterns—like hand-cut leaves and torn edges. She chose patterned papers in varying shades and tints of brown for her background, allowing for the bit of color in the digitally enhanced photo to pop.

Supplies: Cardstock; patterned paper (BasicGrey, Daisy D's); letter stickers (American Crafts); stamps (Sugarloaf); stipple brush (Tsukineko); photo action by Valerie Foster (Do You Digi); Misc: adhesive, ink, pen

When working with neutrals, you aren't limited to one color. On this page, I used various shades of white, cream and brown to make an interesting backdrop for colorful photos. Neutral colors are perfect for framing brightly colored images; neutrals don't compete visually and can make the other colors appear even brighter.

Supplies: Cardstock; transparency (Hambly); chipboard letter (Heidi Swapp); chipboard shapes (Everlasting Keepsakes); heart (Heidi Grace); heart brad (Making Memories); Misc: adhesive, blank certificate, floss, ink, pen, vellum

YOUR CHALLENGE

Create a page that uses neutral shades from different color groups.

contagious laughter

when you laugh everyone laughs with you. You laugh with your whole person & people respond to it.

you @ 30

JUNE 1 · 07

Black and white look stunning with both black-and-white and color photos. When using black and white, try including shades of gray along with a variety of patterns and textures to unify the two colors and bring your page to life. You really can't go wrong with black and white; the combination will only serve to enhance your photos and create a timeless look.

Supplies: Patterned paper (CherryArte, Rouge de Garance); plastic letters (Maya Road); letter stickers (American Crafts); tag (Every Jot & Tittle); Misc: adhesive, button, floss, pen

YOUR CHALLENGE
Create a page using black, white and shades of gray.

it's funny that it's rare to find a photo of the two of us. you would think with me always having a camera in hand there would be lots but this photo is a year old & there is not a more recent one to be found. this is something i've got to remedy 'cause when we're old i want to see how how good we looked! young & oh so happy!!

you & me

october 2006 photo taken at sunset on the beach. a moment stolen away during thanksgiving in sarnia.

You may not have thought to mix white and cream because it seems contrary to rules about matching. But once you see the combination, you realize its potential. This layout's use of white and cream, along with various textures, creates a quietly stunning backdrop for my photo and helps achieve the soft look I wanted for this page.

Supplies: Cardstock; transparency (Hambly); chipboard letters (BasicGrey); 3D gloss (Ranger); Misc: adhesive, craft foam, felt, floss, paint, pen

YOUR CHALLENGE
Create a page using only cream and white elements.

✔ Create Foam Buttons
You will need: Paper punches, craft foam, pencil, leather hole punch

1 Use paper punches to punch various shapes from the craft foam.

2 Mark two or four dots in the center of each shape with the pencil.

3 Punch holes, using the pencil marks as guides, into the foam shapes with the leather hole punch.

 Note: For this project, you can use a ⅛" (32mm) hole punch or other sharp object to make the holes in the foam. But note that the hole sizes will be different than with a leather hole punch I used and may change the look of the buttons.

Colors on a scrapbook page should be the same value

When describing a color, people will usually make references to how dark or light the color is. This is known as the color's value. When choosing colors to use together, the obvious choice is to choose colors that have the same value. For example, when choosing a pale green you match it with a light blue. But what happens when you break free of this rule? Instantly, colors gain new life because of the contrast created. The farther apart the values are, the more contrast you will create. Whether you choose a mid-range value and a darker one or high-contrast dark and light, drama is yours for the making. How far you choose to take this concept is up to you.

High contrast—dark and light—makes for a striking layout. On this page, the color coordination is particularly successful because the pale blue accent color has tones of the deep purple background. When pairing colors with different values, look for a shade of the light color that has a reflection of the dark color in it to help unify the colors.

Supplies: Cardstock; transparency (Hambly); letter stickers (American Crafts); Misc: adhesive, circle punch, pen, staples

YOUR CHALLENGE

Create a page using colors of different intensities, choosing a light color that has tones of the dark color in it.

It took me a minute to figure out what you meant when you asked this question. You wanted to climb the old pine tree in the backyard—no pineapples

can we climb the **pineapple tree?**

involved! After a good laugh off we went to give you a chance to climb. For the very time you were able to climb the low branches by yourself making you a good pineapple tree climber! 07-03-05

If you're not sure where to start, look for patterned paper with colors in contrasting intensities. When you rely on the designer's expertise, the complicated work will be done for you. On the paper I chose for this layout, the designer paired lighter shades of blue-gray with a dark olive green. I picked out the green to use as my solid color so it would contrast with the mostly pale background.

Supplies: Cardstock; patterned paper (BasicGrey); letter stickers (American Crafts); chipboard shape (Everlasting Keepsakes); buttons (SEI); Misc: adhesive, paint, pen

YOUR CHALLENGE

Choose a patterned paper for your page that incorporates colors with two different intensities.

I smile whenever I look at you.

TRÈS JOLIE

Artwork by Michelle Guray

If highly contrasting colors don't appeal to you or they don't match the mood of your page, take note of Michelle's layout. The mid-range orange and the pale blue-green have different intensities, but the contrast between them is not as great. Contrast doesn't have to be jarring to be effective and break the rules. A small amount of contrast works beautifully.

Supplies: Cardstock; patterned paper (Crate Paper, My Mind's Eye); digital brush by Nancie Rowe Janitz (ScrapArtist); felt trim (Queen & Co.); flowers (Making Memories, Prima); gems (K&Co.); paper trim (Doodlebug); photo turn (7gypsies); rub-ons (Hambly); Misc: adhesive, brads, pen, thread

PAGE PERFECTION:
The Rules of Page Layout

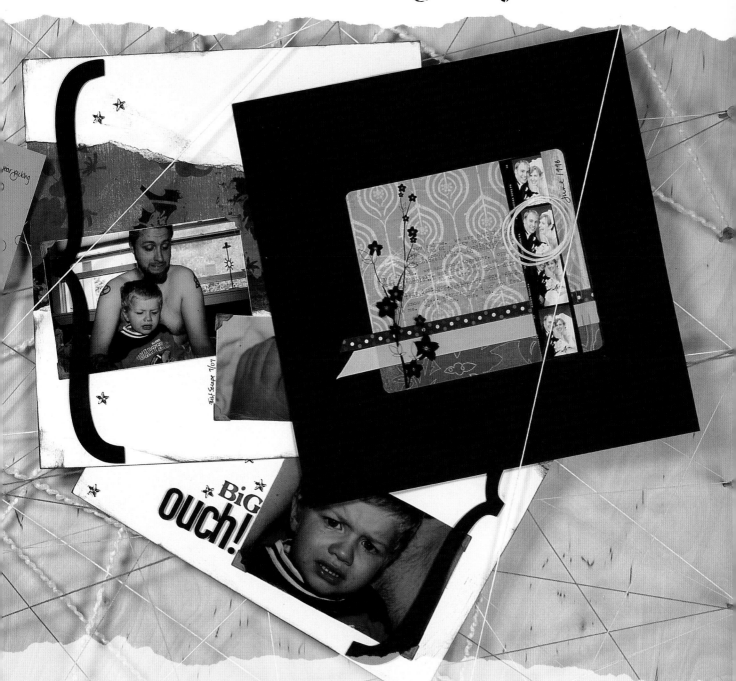

How you arrange items on your pages is just as important as what items you include.
The arrangement of elements doesn't just affect the look of your layout. It also affects the clarity of
your message and the readability of your page. Scrapbookers have adopted certain graphic design
concepts as rules for creating attractive pages. These principles of design—like using visual triangles
and creating symmetry—provide structure and harmony, but that doesn't mean you can't relax
them and create attractive designs in different ways. Like all rules, page layout rules should be your
foundation and not your boundaries. The key to effectively breaking the rules of page layout lies in
your ability and willingness to look beyond the easy and the obvious.

Avoid using a grid to design a page because grids are boring

Think of a layout as a building project that requires a framework. The framework of a page is often the part you will spend the most time on because it provides structure for your layout, like a framework provides for a building. Grids can give you a solid framework for your design and enable you to quickly and easily decide on the placement of elements. Grids are wonderful design tools, but they don't have to be used as is. In other words, a series of boring squares doesn't have to be the end result of a grid-based page. Like other boundaries, grids are just a guide. Let your imagination lead you to alter a grid for pages that really cut loose.

YOUR CHALLENGE

Create a page using a grid structure, but combine sections of the grid when placing elements.

Here, Anilu created a page that is clearly based on a grid, yet is anything but dull and boring. By combining sections of the grid and limiting the grid space to the center of the layout, Anilu created a clean, simple yet engaging page showcasing her photos. Think of grids as tools that you can alter to suit your needs while still giving your page structure.

Supplies: Cardstock; patterned paper (KI Memories); die-cut letters (QuicKutz); brads (Around the Block); Misc: adhesive

Artwork by Anilu Magloire

make me **smile**

For visual punch, try turning your grid on an angle as I did here. Making this slight change has a major impact, creating an untraditional but structured look. For added interest and movement, I attached groupings of photos and embellishments, letting items extend past the grid's perimeters.

Supplies: Cardstock; patterned paper (American Crafts, BasicGrey, October Afternoon); die-cut letter (My Mind's Eye); flower (Blueye Dezines); rub-ons (October Afternoon); ribbon (Stemma); stamps (Gel-a-tins, Technique Tuesday); chipboard shapes (American Crafts); silver crown, stars and wings, vintage seed packs (Papier Valise); Misc: adhesive, cherry bead, heart, staples, transparency squares, tulle

YOUR CHALLENGE
Create a layout with a grid on a 45° angle.

At first glance, it may not seem that a grid is part of the structure for this layout about my husband. But upon a closer look, the 4 × 4 grid (four rows by four columns)—created by the green paper and two orange papers—becomes visible. I used this grid to decide the placement of the orange papers; the polka dot paper spans two columns while the lighter paper spans two rows. A background grid gives a page structure while allowing you to create a design without restraint.

Supplies: Patterned paper (BasicGrey, CherryArte, Prima); letter stickers (American Crafts); stamps (Gel-a-tins); Misc: adhesive, ink, pen

YOUR CHALLENGE
Create a page with a 4 × 4 grid for the background, placing elements that extend past these boundaries.

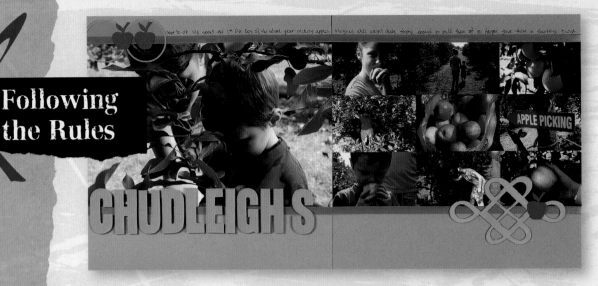

Supplies: Cardstock; chipboard accents (Everlasting Keepsakes); ribbon (Offray); letter stamps (Gel-a-tins); transparency (Hambly); apples (artist's own design); Misc: paint, pen

Both of these two-page layouts utilize a 6 × 3 grid, but there is a decided difference between them. On the layout that follows the rules I did little to alter the grid. But with just a few changes, the layout that breaks the rules gains a lot of visual interest. Reducing the size of the grid helps balance out the busyness of the photos. Replacing the rectangular shapes with circles gives the grid a fresh look, yet still provides structure.

Breaking
the Rules

→

YOUR CHALLENGE
Create a page using a grid, replacing rectangular elements with circles.

Supplies: Cardstock; chipboard accents (Everlasting Keepsakes); ribbon (Offray); letter stamps (Gel-a-tins); transparency (Hambly); doodle template (Crafter's Workshop); apples (artist's own design); Misc: paint, pen

Create a Raised Circle Grid

You will need: 2 sheets of cardstock, ruler, pencil, needle or paper piercer, circle cutter, photos, adhesive foam

Draw a grid on the wrong side of the top piece of cardstock. Follow these directions to make the grid: Draw three horizontal lines. Draw the first horizontal line 2⅜" (6cm) from the top; draw the second horizontal line 2¾" (7cm) below the first line; draw the third horizontal line 2¾" (7cm) below the second line. Then draw three vertical lines. Draw the first vertical line 4¾" (12cm) from the left edge of the page; draw the second vertical line 2¾" (7cm) to the right of the first line; draw the third vertical line 2¾" (7cm) to the right of the second line.

Poke holes with a needle or paper piercer where the lines intersect.

Line up the holes with the point on the circle cutter and cut circles. They should be 2½" (6cm) in diameter. Before proceeding to the next step, decorate the front of the page as desired.

Mark the placement of the circles on the right side of the back piece of cardstock. Use the circle marks as a guide for attaching the photos.

Apply adhesive foam to the wrong side of the top sheet of cardstock, making sure to support the bridges between the circles. Adhere the grid to the cardstock with the photos.

Don't leave empty space on a scrapbook page because it will look unfinished

Empty space on a page can seem scary at first. Your brain tells you to fill, fill, fill. And with all the photos you have and all the fun embellishments at your disposal, filling a page almost seems a necessity. Before you succumb to your mind's requests, take a moment to decide if it's really necessary. Empty space—often called white space—can make a page perfectly complete. It gives your design room to breathe and allows for a page that is less cramped, cluttered and overwhelming.

he's (my) geek & i love him!

funny how i expect you to know the answer to my every question. The thing is if i ask of you... answer. You are like a walking dictionary & in my opinion seem to know everything. i don't know how you do it but it is something i admire.

august 2007

Here, I filled the empty space with subtle patterns. While the patterns aren't technically "white" space, they work effectively for the purpose of creating a space free of elements. When choosing patterned paper to act as white space, pick patterns that are simple in design and limited in color.

Supplies: Cardstock; patterned paper (My Mind's Eye, Prima, Tinkering Ink); letter stickers (American Crafts); chipboard letters (KI Memories); Misc: adhesive, pen

YOUR CHALLENGE
Create a layout using patterned paper as white space.

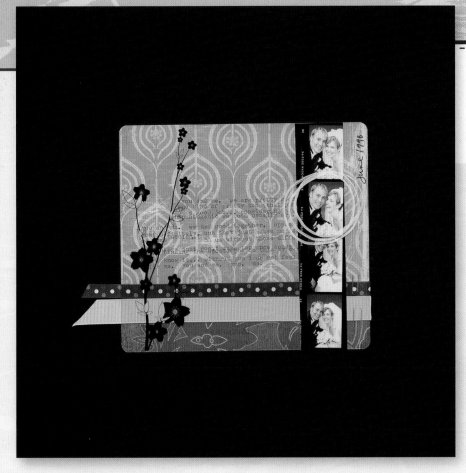

Artwork by Erin Derkatz

YOUR CHALLENGE

Use empty space on a page to form a border around the focus of your layout.

This layout effectively uses empty space to form a border around the main part of the page. By designing her page like this, Erin directs the viewer's eye toward the embellished central part of the page. When creating a page with white space, keep in mind that even though the space is empty, it should still serve a purpose.

Supplies: Cardstock; patterned paper (BasicGrey, Crate Paper); digital brush by Jason Gaylor (Designfruit); ribbon (American Crafts); Misc: adhesive, pen, staples, transparency

The empty space in this design helps the viewer to focus immediately on the photo and journaling. When creating a design such as this, carefully balance any untouched space against the other parts of the page. Here, a wide white strip balances against the empty blue. And a strip of pink felt unifies the elements across the page.

Supplies: Cardstock; plastic letters (Heidi Swapp); letter stickers (Arctic Frog); felt trim (Blueye Dezines); heart (Melissa Frances); staple bar (EK Success); Misc: adhesive, pen

YOUR CHALLENGE

Create a page with at least half of the space on the page empty.

artemis has the most amazing spelling talent. You can spell any word at the very second You are done she can tell you what it is. no hesitating - nothing! and no adult can beat her.

speller extraordinaire
...age 7...

20
RULE

You should use symmetry to create visual balance on a scrapbook page

Balance—equal visual weight—is an important part of good design, and symmetry is an obvious way to achieve it. A symmetrical design is balanced because both sides of a symmetrical page are the same, creating equal visual weight. Symmetry is easy to achieve; you just replicate a design on both sides of a page. But as easy as symmetrical pages are, let's be honest: They can be stiff and boring. The good news is you can still achieve balance by breaking free of symmetry. Asymmetrical designs may take a bit more effort as you learn to recognize less obvious ways to create visual balance—like utilizing color—but it will be well worth the effort.

Artwork by Ronee Parsons

This two-page scrapbook layout uses large brackets to create some sense of symmetry. But the large red slashes of patterned paper and the placement of the photos pushes the design from symmetrical to asymmetrical. When creating a page with an asymmetrical design, you don't have throw all sense of symmetry out the window.

Supplies: Cardstock; patterned paper (BasicGrey); letter stickers (American Crafts, BasicGrey); chipboard accent (Everlasting Keepsakes); star nail heads (Papier Valise); Misc: adhesive, ink

YOUR CHALLENGE
Create an asymmetrical page with some items placed symmetrically.

YOUR CHALLENGE

Create a layout that balances a
large photo with other elements.

With the larger photo placed on one side of the page and the larger orange shape placed on the opposite side, this page achieves balance. In addition, the visual weight of the page is near the bottom, which is balanced by the empty space at the top. When creating balance on an asymmetrical page, consider the weight of items from top to bottom as well as left to right.

Supplies: Cardstock; letter stickers (American Crafts); paper flowers (Blueye Dezines); gems (Westrim); Misc: adhesive, felt, floss, pen

Following the Rules

It's evident that the page that breaks the rules radiates more energy than the layout the follows the rules. The lively, asymmetrical design matches the mood of the page and adds to the look of the photos more effectively than the symmetrical design. A simple way to balance an asymmetrical design is to place most of the items on one side of the page, leaving the other side nearly empty. Then ground the design by adding a connecting element, like the yellow horizontal line here.

Supplies: Patterned paper (Prima, Upsy Daisy); letter stickers (BasicGrey); rub-ons (Hambly, Melissa Frances); buttons (SEI); Misc: adhesive, felt, pen, staples

Breaking the Rules

YOUR CHALLENGE
Create a layout with elements grouped on one side, using a line of color to ground the design.

teaching scrappin' in texas.

Camiller

Smoothie enjoyed at the airport after a busy weekend of

a blueberry & honey

Pure
BLISS

june '07

Here, I used both vertical and horizontal lines to ground the asymmetrical design. Most of the visual weight lies where the two lines intersect, so I placed the page's title in the opposite corner for balance. To create balance, examine your page to determine where the most visual weight lies, and then place other elements opposite that location.

Supplies: Cardstock; letter stickers (Making Memories); transparency frame (My Mind's Eye); chipboard shapes (CherryArte); flowers (Heidi Grace); felt trim (Blueye Dezines); heart (Melissa Frances); Misc: adhesive, floss, ink, lace, pen, rickrack, staples

YOUR CHALLENGE

Create a page with items grouped to one side using elements on the opposite sides to balance the visual weight.

RULE 21

You should use a visual triangle to create movement on a layout

Visual movement is the path the eye follows around a page. Without movement, the eye gets trapped in one area and the message gets lost. One of the most common ways to create movement is with a triangle highlighting three points around the page. For example, you might repeat a color in three spots or include three similar embellishments. As with other design concepts, there is more than one way to create visual movement. So try something new. And remember, new doesn't necessarily mean hard. Many of the methods for creating visual movement rely on a simple left to right or top to bottom movement, which plays off of years of training your eye to read. Time to get moving!

YOUR CHALLENGE
Use a photo on a page that has visual lines and extend them with paper or embellishments.

Artwork by Jeniece Tackett

By placing all the page embellishments on the same angled line as the swing, Jeniece has enhanced the sense of movement in the photo. This choice creates a path for the eye to follow, drawing the eye across the entire page. When creating movement, look for lines in your photo that can be extended with embellishments.

Supplies: Cardstock; patterned paper (Daisy D's); chipboard letters (American Crafts); transparent frame (My Mind's Eye); label sticker (Martha Stewart); rub-ons (Sassafras Lass); stamps (Karen Foster); Misc: adhesive, brads, ink, pen

A rapid succession of photos taken of a person in action will show movement if you line up the photos, as Janine has here. Add to this some carefully placed arrows to move the eye along the line of photos, and the page has all the necessary movement for a lively layout.

Artwork by Janine Langer

Supplies: Cardstock; chipboard shapes, patterned paper (Scenic Route); letter stickers (American Crafts); button, sticker accent (7gypsies); arrow (Heidi Swapp); digital label by Jennifer Pebbles (Two Peas in a Bucket); transparency (Hambly); Misc: adhesive, ink, pen

Journaling Translation
One of your characteristics I admire most is your ability to stand up and try it again if something goes wrong.

YOUR CHALLENGE
Create a page that uses arrows to enhance repetetive elements.

The sequential photos of my daughter skipping rope have all been cropped to the same size to create repetition. The repetition and placement along a bouncing line creates movement on the page that draws the eye through the visual story. Also, the graduated strips of cream cardstock pull the eye down the page to the title.

Supplies: Cardstock; patterned paper (October Afternoon); chipboard letters (Crate Paper); stamp (Dollarstore); Misc: adhesive, ink

YOUR CHALLENGE

Create a layout that uses repetition of size, color or embellishments to communicate movement.

YOUR CHALLENGE

Create a page that uses
a step-like movement.

This page uses a step-like movement—left to right and top to bottom—that comes naturally to most people after years of reading. Angling the photos from the top left corner to the bottom right corner helps the eye follow a natural movement through the page. And placing a color photo at the top and again at the bottom of the page guides the viewer from one focal point to another.

Supplies: Cardstock; patterned paper (Rouge de Garance); letter stickers (American Crafts); gems (Gel-a-tins); rub-ons (Upsy Daisy); Misc: adhesive, pen

This layout illustrates radial movement, where elements appear to rotate from a center point or swirl along a circular path. Here, I cut the patterned paper into triangular shapes that radiate from the center of the page. Then I placed the photos in a pinwheel formation and the arrows and title on the same circular path to lead the eye around the page.

Supplies: Patterned paper (Crate Paper, SEI); letter stickers (Arctic Frog); arrow (American Crafts); gems (Gel-a-tins); paper star (Prima); Misc: adhesive, felt, pen

YOUR CHALLENGE

Create a page that uses
radial movement.

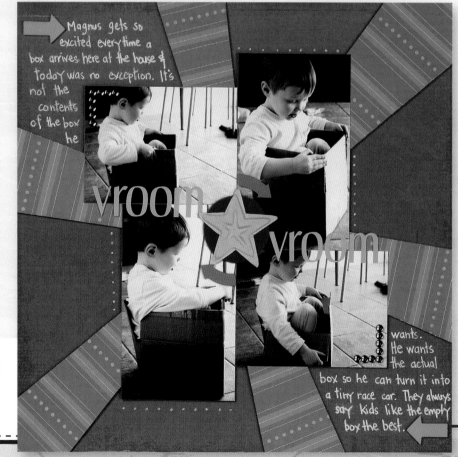

Only beginners should create simple scrapbook pages

Simplicity can be deceiving. Take the little black dress: It's simple in design, but elegant and flattering. A simple scrapbook page is like the little black dress. It doesn't mean boring, plain or even easy. When a simple design is used, you notice every detail, and the focal point stands out. Every potential element needs to be scrutinized to determine if it adds to the design or makes it too busy. It can be hard to break the habit of overloading a page with embellishments. When breaking this rule, keeping in mind a few tips—such as limiting your colors and using simple patterns—will help you achieve a solidly simple design.

hand talker *must be the french canadian!*

YOUR CHALLENGE

Create a page that uses black-and-white photos, a limited color scheme and a reduced number of page embellishments.

Here, each element contributes to the harmony needed to make a successful simple page. While simple, this page took a lot of thought to create. Each item was carefully chosen for a reason: The title is balanced by the sticker, the photos are balanced by the large expanse of untouched pattern, the ribbon acts as a ground for the design, and the warm fuchsia color adds contrast to the cool blue.

Supplies: Patterned paper, ribbon, sticker (SEI); chipboard letters (CherryArte); Misc: adhesive, paint, pen

Me and my girl

watching the airplanes and birds go by.

Artwork by Michelle Guray

Here, Michelle used symmetry to create a simple design. The solid background, a limited color palette and few embellishments all help create balance on the page. When making a simple layout, it's helpful to limit your supply choices so you reduce the possibility of overwhelming your page.

Supplies: Cardstock; brad (K&Co.); butterfly (ARTchix); flowers (Jenni Bowlin); gems (Doodlebug); Misc: adhesive, pen

I wanted this page to be simple so the message to my mother would stand out. To produce a cohesive, uncomplicated page, I employed similar colors and shapes. I used paper from the same collection, and repeated rounded edges. Keep in mind that when creating a simple page, repeating elements will help you avoid complicating your design.

Supplies: Patterned paper (K&Co.); letter stickers (Arctic Frog); vintage sequin (Papier Valise); Misc: adhesive, pen

YOUR CHALLENGE
Create a simple page design using repeating colors and techniques.

for every part of your life that you have given me i am

grateful

2007

chapter

6

grand.ma

loves you

so much

SUPPLY HAPPY:
The Rules About Supplies

Even though you buy scrapbook supplies with every intention of being creative with them, you probably still follow rules about how to use them. Add to this a mental list of what are considered "scrapbook supplies" and you are limited even more. Many of the rules regarding supplies concern paper. The more options you have, the more you follow the rules so you are not overwhelmed by it all. Rules help you use paper the "right" way. But if you look at your supplies as a blank canvas with no preconceived ideas of how to use them, you free yourself from the boundaries created by their labels. Pushing yourself to use new supplies or old supplies in new ways will open up a floodgate of ideas that will have you scrapping with new vigor.

Patterned paper must match

Choosing patterned papers can be an intimidating task. You need to coordinate not only colors, but patterns and sometimes textures, too. It's no wonder you play it safe and choose papers that match, often using papers from the same collection. It's such a simple, time-saving technique, it's almost too tempting to ignore. But following the rules in this way doesn't actually teach you anything. In fact, it leaves you with no idea how to coordinate miscellaneous papers in your stash, and it doesn't always allow for the most interesting page. Once you have an idea of how to mix patterns, you will be able to coordinate them in ways that don't match in the traditional sense but that still work well together on a page.

inside & out

beautiful

december 2006

YOUR CHALLENGE
Use two contrasting patterns in limited colors on a layout.

The wild difference between these two patterns is actually what makes them work together. The series of contrasts creates balance on the page. The clean, crisp geometric pattern balances the soft, distressed floral. The overscale flower balances the small circles. And the limited colors in each pattern keep the contrast from becoming too overwhelming.

Supplies: Patterned paper (Crate Paper, SEI); letter stickers (American Crafts); trim (Wal-Mart); Misc: adhesive, pen

TODAY

You had to act like a monkey while I was trying to take your picture. You are truly a silly girl! Spring 2006

YOUR CHALLENGE

Choose three patterned papers with at least one shared color and crop them to the same size to use on your page.

This page shows one of the simplest ways to coordinate patterned papers. Jeniece chose a plaid, a dot and an abstract floral that use shared colors and then cropped them to the same shape and size. By giving all the patterns this same treatment, she created consistency and unity between the paper designs.

Supplies: Patterned paper (Daisy D's, My Mind's Eye, Sassafras Lass, We R Memory Keepers); chipboard letters, journaling tag, letter stickers, scalloped tape (Heidi Swapp); rickrack (Fancy Pants); transparency (Hambly); buttons (Color It); chipboard flower (American Crafts): Misc: adhesive, staples

even though you guys are seven years apart

there couldn't be a closer bond between the

two of you. you are both so happy in each

other's company. siblings and best friends.

summer, 2006

harper & magnus

7 years

This page features three patterned papers that traditionally would not be mixed. But they work well on this page because the scale of the three patterns varies and the amount of each pattern I used also varies. Both techniques create visual interest, encouraging the eye to move around the page. Plus, the blue-and-yellow color scheme ties the patterns together.

Supplies: Cardstock; patterned paper (CherryArte, Prima); brackets (BasicGrey); heart (American Crafts); number tag (Every Jot & Tittle); ribbon (Fancy Pants); Misc: adhesive, paint, pen, staples

YOUR CHALLENGE
Create a page that features varying amounts of three patterns, and tie them together with color.

swimming

At the end of every school year the entire school takes lessons at the community swimming pool.

level 14

Not only is it a great thing that every child learns to swim but the kids get to end the year with something fun.

lessons

June 19, 2007

This page uses a whopping 15 different patterned papers, yet the overall look is unified. Try the simple trick I used here when creating a row of patterns: Take one color from the first pattern and choose the next pattern using this color as its base. Repeat this, making sure each pattern carries a color from the previous pattern. Here, cutting papers into strips of a similar size helps unify the wide array of patterns and colors.

Supplies: Cardstock; patterned paper (BasicGrey, Crate Paper, Heidi Grace, KI Memories, Prima, SEI); letter stickers (American Crafts); Misc: adhesive, pen

→

YOUR CHALLENGE

Create a page with a row of patterns that carries colors from one paper to the next.

Using neutrals makes pattern mixing easy. By their very nature, neutrals go with anything, as illustrated here by Ronee's page. Both the notebook and the brown wallpaper-inspired paper are neutral in color, providing an impartial background for the more colorful paper.

Supplies: Software (Abode); digital patterned paper by Carla Gibson (Oscraps), Catrine (Catscrap), (Lazar Studiowerx); brushes by Michelle Coleman and Nancy Rowe Janitz (ScrapArtist); labels, tears by Vicki Stegall (Oscraps)

YOUR CHALLENGE

Combine a neutral-colored patterned paper with a colorful patterned paper on a scrapbook page.

This is what I get for leaving my makeup bag in your room. A huge mess on the floor, and on your face

UP Make

Man

but you do look pretty cute.

08/2007

Artwork by Ronee Parsons

24 RULE

Use bold patterns only in small portions

Do you love large, bold patterned papers, but shy away from using them? It's true that bold patterns can be intimidating. It's definitely easier to follow the rules and use only small amounts (or none at all) than to risk overpowering a photo. Like most things in life, successfully using bold patterns is all about balance. And balance requires careful planning. Whether you choose to counter bold patterns with equally lively photos or minimize embellishments to let the paper shine, using bold patterns successfully is within your reach. Are you up for the challenge?

Artwork by Erin Derkatz

Erin's page is another example of how creating contrast provides balance for a page. Here a piece of busy patterned paper contrasts with the calm and peaceful nature of the oversized photo. This contrast draws the eye in to rest on the special picture.

Supplies: Cardstock; patterned paper (Autumn Leaves, BasicGrey); ribbon (BasicGrey, Cosmo Cricket); brad (K&Co.); decorative tape (Making Memories); Misc: adhesive, paint, pen, staples, thread

YOUR CHALLENGE

Create a page that juxtaposes a busy patterned paper with a quiet photo.

YOUR CHALLENGE

Use a bold pattern to form a border around a grouping of black-and-white photos.

06 30 '06

*everytime the camera comes out this what i get!

cheezy

grins

On this page, the bold pattern I used forms a border around the grouping of photos placed at its center. Because this border is visually busy, the eye is drawn to the quieter area of the black-and-white photos. Solid red embellishments help anchor the images.

Supplies: Patterned paper (Tinkering Ink); letter stickers (K&Co.); chipboard arrow (Deluxe Designs); stars (American Crafts); label sticker (Martha Stewart); ribbon (Fancy Pants); Misc: adhesive, paint, pen

Here, Ronee used a simple design and coordinating colors to create an attractive patterned layout. To separate her photo from this busy background, Ronee lifted it with adhesive foam, creating a division between elements. And embellishments with graphic patterns—the circles and grids on the transparencies—provide a welcoming balance to the busy floral.

Supplies: Patterned paper (American Crafts, Hambly); transparency (Hambly); letter stickers (American Crafts); stamps (Gel-a-tins); Misc: adhesive, ink, pen

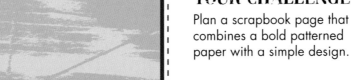

YOUR CHALLENGE

Plan a scrapbook page that combines a bold patterned paper with a simple design.

Following
the Rules

On the layout that follows the rules, the bold pattern is nearly lost behind the photos. In fact, the photos are almost lost as well. The competition for attention between the photos and pattern pushes the eye to run for the expanse of the empty blue paper. The other layout shows how breaking the rules brings attention to the photos. This page incorporates a large piece of bold pattern that balances the photos on the right. The pattern works with the page design, not against it.

Breaking
the Rules

YOUR CHALLENGE
Design a page using a bold pattern as a tool to create balance on your page.

2.5 RULE

A two-page layout should use the same background paper for each page

When starting a two-page layout, you likely search through your stash for two identical papers. After all, you think, a two-page spread still acts as one page, so both pages should have the same background. Not so! To make a successful two-page layout, there needs to be a sense of cohesiveness between the two sides. But there are many ways, besides using twin papers, to make both pages look like they belong together. You can unite the sides with color or embellishments, or have photos or a title cross the layout's gutter. By breaking this rule your pages are sure to stand out.

(TOOMIE)

every night at dinner magnus would talk about his friend toomie. we were stumped until one night at dinner we noticed magnus watching his reflection in the kitchen DATE jan '07 window. when he looked at the window panes he could see two reflections so he dubbed them... two-me!

For this layout, I started with two papers from the same collection to ensure a unified background. But it's the title and photos that really bring the sides together. The photos' central placement, along with their mirrored look, make them appear as one that spans the spread. Placing the title similarly—across the gutter—has the same effect.

YOUR CHALLENGE

Create a two-page layout using papers from the same collection for the layout's background.

Supplies: Cardstock; die-cut shapes, patterned paper (CherryArte); chipboard letters (Crate Paper); 3-D gloss (Ranger); Misc: adhesive, paint, pen

YOUR CHALLENGE
Create a two-page layout with different background papers and a colored border.

This layout works well because both papers use the same color tones. Matching embellishments in opposite corners also help unify the design. Try crossing colored borders over the gutter, as I did, to connect the sides.

Supplies: Cardstock; patterned paper (Fancy Pants, My Mind's Eye); chipboard letters (CherryArte); chipboard shapes, letter stickers (American Crafts); rub-ons (Crate Paper); tag (Every Jot & Tittle); transparency (Hambly); Misc: adhesive, buttons, paint, pen

Artwork by Michelle Guray

YOUR CHALLENGE
On a two-page layout, use two papers, carrying a piece of one to the other side.

Different elements unify Michelle's layout. The positive and negative versions of the pattern—red with ivory dots and ivory with red dots—and the sliver of red paper that carries over from the left make it clear the halves are one page.

Supplies: Cardstock; patterned paper (Daisy D's, Jenni Bowlin); chipboard letters (Heidi Swapp); flowers (Prima); stamp (October Afternoon); stickers (7gypsies, Making Memories); Misc: adhesive, brads, ink

RULE 26

Use only supplies intended for scrapbooking

Get your archival spray ready for this one! Not every page you create needs to last a lifetime. This is a hard rule to break if you are a hardcore archivist. But what is a hobby if you can't play every once in a while? There are a variety of goodies that work wonderfully on scrapbook pages that are not sold in the scrapbooking aisle. Of course, I'm not suggesting you try breaking this rule with priceless photos that require acid-free products. But feel free to have fun with not-so-great shots (and see Chapter 2!) or digital photos. The freedom that comes with shaking off this rule will keep you coming back for more.

Vintage items are a great way to enhance a page's theme as well as bring in something different. Here, a vintage baby ointment label and an old torn picture book cover help illustrate the childhood theme. I also included bug-shaped beads to add a boyish look.

Supplies: Cardstock; chipboard shapes (Everlasting Keepsakes); embossing glitter, gems, stamps (Gel-a-tins); chipboard letters (American Crafts); ladybug beads, vintage label (Papier Valise); rhinestone flourish (Prima); transparency frame (My Mind's Eye); Misc: adhesive, letter stickers, paint, pen, vintage book cover

YOUR CHALLENGE
Mix some vintage items with traditional scrap supplies on a page.

This page employs a variety of unusual items to provide interest and texture. Both the orange mesh and packaging used as a circular stamp were rescued from the trash. I purchased fusible thread, not for sewing but specifically for scrapping. Along with these items, tags and graph paper from the office supply store and items from the craft store work to create a one-of-a-kind page.

Supplies: Patterned paper (BasicGrey, Crate Paper, KI Memories); clear letters (Heidi Swapp); ribbon (Masterstroke); vintage sequins (Papier Valise); Misc: adhesive, cotton string, craft foam, decorative scissors, graph paper, mesh, pen, staples, tags

YOUR CHALLENGE
Use a found object to create a one-of-a-kind accent or backdrop for your page.

YOUR CHALLENGE
Use a piece of memorabilia that ties into the story on your layout.

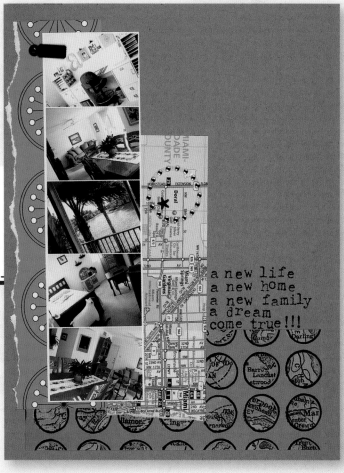

Memorabilia seems to have gone by the wayside in scrapbooking, but Anilu has used it quite effectively on this page. By using a piece of a city map that marks the location of her new house, she ties the page accents to her story in a way no scrapbook product could.

Supplies: Cardstock; patterned paper (Fontwerks, Urban Lily); photo turn (7gypsies); rhinestone accent (Heidi Swapp); Misc: adhesive, ink, map, stamps

Artwork by Anilu Magloire

Look no further than that empty box of supplies to add elements to your page. On this layout Janine used corrugated cardboard to make custom embellishments. Using cardboard is a great way to recycle what you already have, and it adds texture and dimension. Use it to add a masculine look or to contrast feminine elements, like sweet buttons and bird-shaped felt, as Janine did here.

Supplies: Cardstock; patterned paper (BasicGrey); letter stickers (American Crafts, Heidi Swapp); buttons (Autumn Leaves); digital label by Jennifer Pebbles (Two Peas in a Bucket); felt bird (Jenni Bowlin); ribbon (May Arts); transparency (Hambly); Misc: adhesive, cardboard, ink, paint, pen

Artwork by Janine Langer

Journaling Translation
You aren't small anymore. To the contrary, you became a wonderful and enchanting young lady.

YOUR CHALLENGE
Create a page using cardboard or other recycled materials.

A favourite way to spend the day — me, my camera & nature. It is not something I get to do very often 'cause life is busy but it just makes these times more special.

* Photos taken at the Butterfly Conservatory

Feb. 07

JUST ...ME... & my CAMERA

To create this page I chose several items that aren't scrapping supplies— a flocked T-shirt transfer, handmade pom-poms, a paper doily and dollar store letters. All of these items got my creative juices flowing since they were so different from what I normally use. And the time I spent on this page gave me some much needed relaxation with a hobby I love.

Supplies: Cardstock; doily; letter stickers (Dollarstore); flock transfer (Plaid); ribbon stiff (Strano); ribbon (Fancy Pants); rub-ons (My Mind's Eye); stamps (Making Memories); Misc: adhesive, floss, ink, paint, pen, staples

YOUR CHALLENGE

Give yourself permission to play and use nontraditional items on a layout about you.

✔ Create a Fun Pom-Pom Embellishment

You will need: Cardboard, transparent tape, embroidery floss, scissors

1 Cut two pieces of cardboard ½" × 2" (1cm × 5cm). Stack the pieces on top of one another and wrap them with transparent tape.

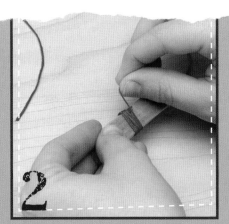

2 Cut a piece of embroidery floss to approximately 8" (20cm) long. Set this aside. Then, wrap the remaining floss around the cardboard, keeping the floss toward the center. Wrap 50–75 times.

3 Carefully slide the floss off the cardboard. Tie the 8" (20cm) piece of floss around the midpoint of the wrapped floss. Carefully cut through the loops at each end. Fluff the floss to create your pom-pom. Trim any uneven threads.

Note: You can vary the size of your pom-pom by changing the width of cardboard. You can vary the fullness of your pom-pom by changing the number of times you wrap the thread around the cardboard.

chapter 7

Have you figured out that breaking the rules is about choosing the options that aren't always easy or safe? It's about getting out of your comfort zone, trying something new and letting the creative juices flow. Handwrite on a page if you never have before, look for new ways to add texture or give digital scrapbooking a try.

And remember, the rules of scrapbooking are not limited to the ones covered in this book. Once you start to become aware of the rules that affect your creative decisions you will start to see just how many there are. First, take some time to learn how to break just a few more random rules. Then get out and cut loose!

RULE 27

You should limit texture on a layout if you want it to be flat

Using dimensional embellishments has become a trend in scrapbooking. You have probably welcomed this trend because of the texture it adds to your scrapbook pages. But then there's the dilemma of the lump and weight that comes with texture, right? Not so. Texture is not only defined by its feel, but also by its appearance. So shiny (and flat) metallic paper can be used for texture just as well as corduroy brads. There are lots of other ways to add flat texture as well. They require moving out of your comfort zone and looking at surfaces in new ways. But adding two-dimensional texture is great way to turn flat into fabulous.

On this layout, Anilu used typical (and flat) scrapbook supplies to add different textures. She chose a textured background cardstock and patterned paper that mimics fabric. She then stamped circles, some of which she heat embossed and some of which she highlighted with glitter, creating sparkly and glossy surfaces. She finished the page with a few spots of felt for soft texture.

Supplies: Cardstock; patterned paper (BasicGrey); felt flowers and letter (American Crafts); stamps (Fontwerks); Misc: adhesive, brads, embossing powder, glitter, ink

YOUR CHALLENGE

Add two textures to a layout using flat scrapbook products.

Artwork by Anilu Magloire

This page is jammed with visual texture, yet has nothing that will get squished in an album. And the contrast between the different kinds of texture—flocked letters and metallic finishes, torn vellum and hand stitches, and mesh layered with tissue paper—all lend excitement to this fun summertime page. When creating texture, try mixing lots of different types to create an unexpected look that begs to be touched.

Supplies: Cardstock; patterned paper (CherryArte, KI Memories, Paper Company); flock (Stampendous); mesh (Magenta); Misc: adhesive, decorative scissors, floss, pen, vellum

YOUR CHALLENGE
Use four to five different types of flat texture on a page.

Erin has added lots of texture to her layout without using anything that gives the page bulk. Glitter, unevenly applied paint, fabric and stitches all give her page texture. To finish off this page, Erin printed her photo, slightly crumpled and distressed it and then tore it along the top edge. The result is a cohesive look, using textures that are rough and worn.

Supplies: Cardstock; mask (Heidi Swapp); ribbon (American Crafts); Misc: adhesive, embossing powder, fabric, notebook paper, paint, pen, staples, thread

YOUR CHALLENGE
Design a layout using worn and rough elements to create flat texture.

Artwork by Erin Derkatz

111

YOUR CHALLENGE
Use a printed transparency over another paper to create texture on your page.

Artwork by Michelle Guray

YOU
ARE

awe·some

1 · inspiring awe or admiration

2 · outstanding, remarkable

Here, Michelle created texture with a smooth, glossy transparency placed over a medium-tooth watercolor paper. The transparency has a messy printed design, and Michelle rubbed paint unevenly over the watercolor paper. Layering a transparency over another paper gives the page the appearance of texture and depth without adding bulk.

Supplies: Patterned paper (CherryArte); transparency (Hambly); letter stickers (Heidi Swapp); word stickers (Making Memories); photo corners (American Crafts); Misc: adhesive, paint, watercolor paper

never a dull moment with you. you are always up for a laugh & always

Top THINGS i love about you

This page features a lot of different textures, but the one with the most impact is the distressed treatment given to the background paper. This simple bone folder embossing technique gives paper texture across the entire page and makes a wonderful backdrop for the other textures. You can create your embossed background from lines like I did here, or you can create a more intricate design.

Supplies: Cardstock; patterned paper (Scenic Route, Upsy Daisy); letter stickers (Making Memories); ribbon (Strano); stamp (Gel-a-tins); Misc: adhesive, cardboard, embossing powder, ink, paint, pen, staples, tag

YOUR CHALLENGE
Design a textural background for your page using bone folder embossing.

✓ Create Embossed Texture

You will need: Colored paper with white core, straightedge, pencil, bone folder or scoring blade, sanding sponge

1 Draw a design on the back side of your paper with pencil. (Tip: If the finished scrapbook page is a two-page spread, make sure the lines cross the page gutter.)

2 With a bone folder, emboss the marked lines. (A scoring blade made for a paper trimmer also works well.)

3 Lightly sand the right side of the paper to make the embossed lines more prominent.

RULE 28

Your handwriting needs to be neat and pretty to be used on a layout

You can avoid using handwriting on your scrapbook pages for many reasons, but not having perfect handwriting doesn't need to be one of them. First of all, we are often our own worst critics, so your handwriting is probably not as bad as you think. Second, imperfect handwriting doesn't take away from the attractiveness of a page; in fact, it adds a personal touch that computer-generated journaling cannot. Handwriting helps connect the viewer to you whether or not your handwriting is neat. If you are uncomfortable with your handwriting, you can use it in small doses on your pages at first, or add it in a hidden pocket. But do add it—future generations will appreciate it, and so will you.

Artwork by Jeniece Tackett

Supplies: Patterned paper (Crate Paper, Making Memories); chipboard letters, heart (Heidi Swapp); letter stickers (Li'l Davis); decorative tape (7gypsies); label sticker (Jenni Bowlin); notebook punch (Stampin' Up); rub-ons (Daisy D's); stamp (Technique Tuesday); transparency (My Mind's Eye); Misc: adhesive, ink, pen

If you are uncomfortable with your handwriting, try Jeniece's clever technique. By writing her journaling in a "to do" list format she makes messy handwriting completely appropriate for the layout. To do lists are often messy scribbles, so handwriting this type of journaling lends authenticity to a page.

YOUR CHALLENGE
Handwrite your journaling in a list on a layout.

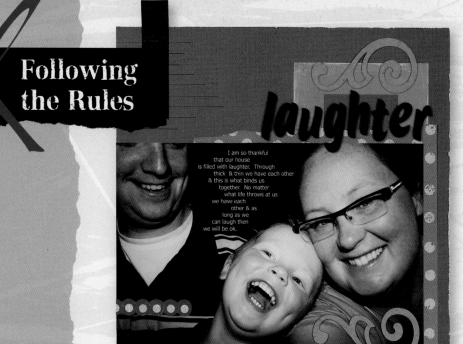

On the layout that follows the rules, the journaling is clear and easy to read because of the computer-generated text. The same message on the layout that breaks the rules reflects a warmth that is lacking in the other layout. My handwriting is certainly not perfect, but since the message was very special I wanted to include a touch that is completely me.

Supplies: Patterned paper (Prima, Upsy Daisy); letter stickers (American Crafts); chipboard shapes (Everlasting Keepsakes); die-cut shapes (Crate Paper); ribbon (Michaels); Misc: adhesive, edge distresser, pen, staples

Breaking the Rules

YOUR CHALLENGE
Include handwritten journaling on a heartfelt page.

Play up messy handwriting on a graffiti-inspired page like this one. Handwriting running in all directions creates a "patterned" background that is not meant to be neat. When creating this look, write on your page in a stream-of-consciousness style, remembering that the messier you are, the more effective the look will be.

Supplies: Cardstock; letter stickers (American Crafts); Misc: adhesive, dimensional paint, floss, foam shapes, pen

YOUR CHALLENGE
Re-create this graffiti-inspired look on a page.

purple piNe coNes

WHILE TAKING A HIKE WITH THE FAMILY WE CAME ACROSS THESE TINY CONES THAT WERE NO BIGGER THAN A DIME.

Stylized journaling is another option for handwriting on your page. By creating a signature font that can be reproduced on any page, you will be able to clearly convey your message in a look that is unique to you without worrying about what your natural handwriting looks like. With a stylized font you can include guidelines, like these wavy ones, that add to the artistry of the page.

Supplies: Patterned paper (Crate Paper, Upsy Daisy); chipboard letters (Heidi Swapp); Misc: adhesive, decorative scissors, pen

YOUR CHALLENGE
Create a page using a stylized handwriting font for the journaling.

✔ Create a Stylized Handwriting Font
You will need: Scrapbook paper, pencil, scrap piece of paper, journaling pen, eraser

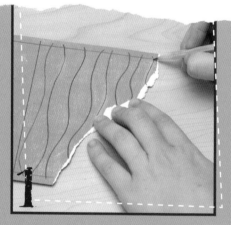

On the printed side of the paper, lightly mark the perimeter of your journaling space. Sketch in the number of wavy guidelines needed. Write out the journaling on a piece of scrap paper.

Using capital letters, add journaling to the lines, making sure both the top and bottom of each letter touch the lines. Take your time when writing letters so they are straight.

Carefully trace the letters and then the wavy lines with a journaling pen. Let the ink dry, and erase any stray pencil marks.

 Note: For variation, leave the guidelines in pencil and erase them, or fill in the guidelines with dots in pen.

RULE 29

Traditional scrapbookers should not make digital pages

If you are a paper scrapper, digital scrapbooking can seem intimidating. So tackle it the same way you did traditional scrapping: Learn one skill at a time, building your skills until you are able to create comfortably. Keep in mind that going digital doesn't mean you have to give up traditional scrapbooking. If you are anything like me you will have a hard time leaving the mess and tactile feeling of paper scrapping behind. But the fun of digital scrapbooking might surprise you. It requires different thought patterns because everything is completely visual, which will stretch you creatively. A major bonus to digital scrapbooking is it leaves you open to experimentation; you won't be wasting or messing up supplies, and the undo button is just a click away.

This appealing digital page requires only a few simple skills and basic word processing or image-editing software. To re-create this page, you need to learn how to drag digital elements onto a page, add text and add a white border to your photos. Once you learn those skills, building the page is just like paper scrapping: add one element at a time until the page is complete.

Supplies; Software (Adobe); digital paper, skull brush, staples by Ronee Parsons (Oscraps); clear letters by Kim Christensen (ScrapArtist); Misc: letter brush

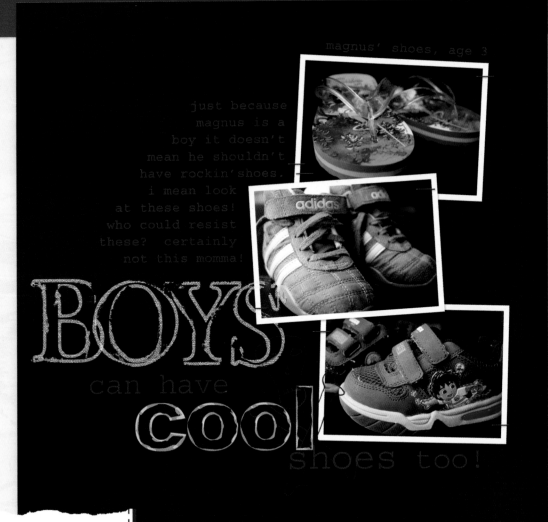

YOUR CHALLENGE
Create a digital page using 2–3 basic skills.

YOUR CHALLENGE
Create a digital page using a digital template.

Digital templates are great tools to use when learning digital scrapbooking. These templates are the equivalent of scrapbook sketches. You simply drop in the digital papers and use the template to "cut" them to size. Also keep in mind that using elements from one digital kit takes the guess work out of the selection process, so you can concentrate on learning new skills.

Supplies: Software (Adobe); digital supplies and template by Ronee Parsons (Oscraps)

Jeniece is not typically a digital scrapper, but she rose to this challenge beautifully. She applied her usual style of paper scrapping to this digital page, using premade digital elements and layering items one at a time. Using digital elements that resemble real-life objects—like cardboard, buttons and doodles—helps you achieve a more traditional look, great for the paper-to-digital transition.

Supplies: Software (Adobe); digital papers (Heather Ann Designs) and Nancy Rowe Janitz (ScrapArtist); distressing kit by Nancy Rowe Janitz (ScrapArtist); doodle frame by Tia Bennett (Two Peas in a Bucket); flower (Heather Ann Designs); journal tag by Kate Teague (Two Peas in a Bucket); word art (Be Audacious); Misc: cardboard

YOUR CHALLENGE
Digitally re-create one of your paper layouts.

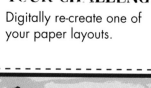

Artwork by Jeniece Tackett

30 RULE

Digital scrapbooking should look the same as paper scrapbooking

It may sound obvious, but it bears repeating: Digital scrapbooking is different from paper scrapping. We should celebrate the difference. Digital has its own beauty that shouldn't be compromised in a quest to mimic paper scrapbooking. Just because it has the word *scrapbooking* in it doesn't mean digital scrapbooking needs to look a certain way. With digital scrapbooking you can create many different effects that are not possible with paper, and you should feel free to explore them. Digital opens up a new method of scrapbooking and new ways to record your memories. Embrace it!

of all the colors in the **rainbow** your favourite is...

There's no denying this page is all digital, no guesswork to determine if elements are real. But it's still a "real" scrapbook page, a lively one that captures life. The spot color in the photograph, the text layered behind my son and the soft edge of the photo all were intentionally used to enhance the digital look. When creating digital pages, cut loose and be true to the art form.

YOUR CHALLENGE
Create a scrapbook page that is distinctly digital.

Supplies: Software (Adobe); digital paper, star trim from O Boy kit (Oscraps)

The beauty of digital scrapbooking is the number of cool effects that can enhance the mood of your page. Here, Ronee played up the quiet mood of the photo by digitally adding a dreamy effect. She layered patterned paper over the photo using the soft light blend mode in an image-editing software program. Her page doesn't look at all traditional, but the moment is captured well.

Supplies: Software (Adobe); digital brush and patterned paper by Ronee Parsons (Oscraps); butterfly, glitter by Sausan Designs (Scrapbook Graphics)

YOUR CHALLENGE

Use a digital effect to enhance the mood of your page.

Artwork by Ronee Parsons

Like Ronee, I chose to use digital effects to enhance the page rather than simply layering embellishments to make the page look traditional. The fading of the central photo into the background paper creates depth that makes it appear as if you could step into the scene. The blending effect also allows for multiple photos to work seamlessly together on the page.

Supplies: Software (Adobe); digital paper, torn paper strips by Chris Ford (Two Peas in a Bucket)

YOUR CHALLENGE

Create a digital page using software to blend photos.

Sunday, May 13, 2007

York Regional Forest

A hike for Mother's Day, all together, enjoying the weather

CONTRIBUTORS

✳ Erin Derkatz

Erin is mom to Sofia and wife to Grant. Together, they reside in Alberta, Canada, where they own a natural health center. Erin loves to "make stuff," so scrapbooking naturally became part of the creative mix. She also loves to laugh, dance, collect cookbooks, explore new places, read and sing in the car.

✳ Michelle Guray

Michelle lives in Southern California with her husband and two children. She discovered scrapbooking more than six years ago and enjoys the hobby immensely, not only as a way to capture memories but as a creative outlet. In her spare time she loves reading magazines, shopping online and going to the movies.

✳ Janine Langer

Janine lives in Solingen, Germany, with her husband, René, and cute little five-year-old monster, Gabriel. She started out as a digital scrapbooker in 2005 but she missed using her hands, and in 2007 she started paper scrapping. She still integrates digital elements on her paper pages, but scrapping with paper is what she really loves. Janine's favorite subject to scrap is her family. And she loves to capture memories—especially her everyday life—trusting that her son will love it when he is old enough to appreciate it. She has met so many beautiful and talented ladies since she started scrapping and she loves being part of such a great international community.

✳ Anilu Magloire

Born in Mexico, Anilu is a devoted scrapbooker living in Miami. She has been married to her husband for almost 10 years and together they have a little four-year-old princess. She fell in love with scrapbooking two years ago and is now hooked for life. Cautious with embellishments, Anilu loves white space and tries to make photos the focus of her pages. This is her first publication and she is still pinching herself.

✳ Ronee Parsons

Ronee lives in Olympia, Washington, with her husband, son and a group of furry four-leggers. Ronee started scrapping in 2004 as a way to document her son's early years and quickly grew passionate about the art. She is a 2007 Memory Makers Master, and more of Ronee's work can be found in her book, *Modern Memory Keeper* (Memory Makers, 2008) and on her blog at roneeparsons.blogspot.com.

✳ Jeniece Tackett

Jeniece has been avidly scrapbooking since her first daughter was born almost six years ago. She is a mother of two: Breana, five, and Savannah, three. She and her husband live on a small farm and enjoy taking care of their home, which has been in the family for four generations. She is a pre-school teacher by day and a scrapbook teacher by night. Jeniece has been teaching scrapbook classes at her local scrapbook store for three years.

Source Guide

The following companies manufacture products featured in this book. Please check your local retailers to find these materials, or go to a company's Web site for the latest product. In addition, we have made every attempt to properly credit the items mentioned in this book. We apologize to any company that we have listed incorrectly, and we would appreciate hearing from you.

Companies with an asterisk (*) generously donated product toward the creation of the artwork in this book.

7gypsies
(877) 749-7797
www.sevengypsies.com

Adobe Systems Incorporated
(800) 833-6687
www.adobe.com

American Crafts
(801) 226-0747
www.americancrafts.com

American Traditional Designs
(800) 448-6656
www.americantraditional.com

ANW Crestwood
(973) 406-5000
www.anwcrestwood.com

Anna Griffin, Inc.
(888) 817-8170
www.annagriffin.com

Arctic Frog
(479) 636-3764
www.arcticfrog.com

Around The Block
(801) 593-1946
www.aroundtheblockproducts.com

ARTchix Studio
(250) 478-5985
www.artchixstudio.com

Autumn Leaves
(800) 588-6707
www.autumnleaves.com

BasicGrey
(801) 544-1116
www.basicgrey.com

Bazzill Basics Paper
(480) 558-8557
www.bazzillbasics.com

Be Audacious
www.audreyneal.com

Berwick Offray, LLC
(800) 344-5533
www.offray.com

Blueye Dezines*
(917) 596-4837
www.blueyedezines.com.au

Bo-Bunny Press
(801) 771-4010
www.bobunny.com

Canson, Inc.
(800) 628-9283
www.canson-us.com

Catscrap
www.catscrap.com

Chatterbox, Inc.
(888) 416-6260
www.chatterboxinc.com

CherryArte*
(212) 465-3495
www.cherryarte.com

Class Act Stamps
www.classact.ca

Clearsnap, Inc.
(888) 448-4862
www.clearsnap.com

Close To My Heart
(888) 655-6552
www.closetomyheart.com

Coats & Clark, Inc.
(800) 648-1479
www.coatsandclark.com

Collage Press
(435) 676-2039
www.collagepress.com

Color It
www.alooman.etsy.com

Cosmo Cricket
(800) 852-8810
www.cosmocricket.com

Crafter's Workshop, The*
(877) 272-3837
www.thecraftersworkshop.com

Crate Paper*
(801) 798-8996
www.cratepaper.com

Creative Imaginations
(800) 942-6487
www.cigift.com

Daisy D's Paper Company
(888) 601-8955
www.daisydspaper.com

Delta Technical Coatings, Inc.
(800) 423-4135
www.deltacrafts.com

Deluxe Designs
(480) 497-9005
www.deluxecuts.com

Designer Digitals
www.designerdigitals.com

Designfruit
www.designfruit.com

Die Cuts With A View
(801) 224-6766
www.diecutswithaview.com

Digital Paper Tearing
www.digitalpapertearing.com

DMC Corp.
(973) 589-0606
www.dmc-usa.com

Do You Digi
www.doyoudigi.com

Dollarstore, Inc.
(949) 261-7488
www.dollarstore.com

Doodlebug Design Inc.
(877) 800-9190
www.doodlebug.ws

EK Success, Ltd.*
(800) 524-1349
www.eksuccess.com

Elmer's Products, Inc.
(800) 848-9400
www.elmers.com

Everlasting Keepsakes*
(816) 896-7037
www.everlastingkeepsakes.com

Every Jot & Tittle
www.everyjotandtittle.etsy.com

Fancy Pants Designs, LLC
(801) 779-3212
www.fancypantsdesigns.com

Fontwerks
(604) 942-3105
www.fontwerks.com

Gel-a-tins*
(800) 393-2151
www.gelatinstamps.com

Glue Dots International
(888) 688-7131
www.gluedots.com

Hambly Screenprints*
(800) 451-3999
www.hamblyscreenprints.com

Heather Ann Designs
www.heatheranndesigns.com

Heidi Grace Designs, Inc.*
(866) 348-5661
www.heidigrace.com

Heidi Swapp/Advantus Corporation*
(904) 482-0092
www.heidiswapp.com

Hero Arts Rubber Stamps, Inc.
(800) 822-4376
www.heroarts.com

Imaginisce
(801) 908-8111
www.imaginisce.com

Impress Rubber Stamps
(206) 901-9101
www.impressrubberstamps.com

Jenni Bowlin
www.jennibowlin.com

Junkitz
(732) 792-1108
www.junkitz.com

K&Company
(888) 244-2083
www.kandcompany.com

Karen Foster Design
(801) 451-9779
www.karenfosterdesign.com

KI Memories
(972) 243-5595
www.kimemories.com

Label Tulip
www.labeltulip.com

Lasting Impressions for Paper, Inc.
(800) 936-2677
www.lastingimpressions.com

Lazar Studiowerx, Inc.
(866) 478-9379
www.lazarstudiowerx.com

Li'l Davis Designs
(480) 223-0080
www.lildavisdesigns.com

Liquitex Artist Materials
(888) 422-7954
www.liquitex.com

Magenta Rubber Stamps
(450) 922-5253
www.magentastyle.com

Making Memories
(801) 294-0430
www.makingmemories.com

Martha Stewart Crafts
www.marthastewartcrafts.com

Marvy Uchida/ Uchida of America, Corp.
(800) 541-5877
www.uchida.com

Masterstroke Canada
www.masterstrokecanada.com

May Arts
(800) 442-3950
www.mayarts.com

Maya Road, LLC
(214) 488-3279
www.mayaroad.com

Melissa Frances/Heart & Home, Inc.*
(888) 616-6166
www.melissafrances.com

Mermaid Tears
(310) 569-3345
www.mermaidtears.net

Michaels Arts & Crafts
(800) 642-4235
www.michaels.com

My Mind's Eye*
(800) 665-5116
www.mymindseye.com

October Afternoon
www.octoberafternoon.com

Offray- see Berwick Offray, LLC

Oscraps
www.oscraps.com

Pageframe Designs
(877) 553-7263
www.scrapbookframe.com

Paper Company, The - see ANW Crestwood

Paper Salon
(800) 627-2648
www.papersalon.com

Paper Source
(888) 727-3711
www.paper-source.com

Papier Valise
(403) 277-1802
www.papiervalise.com

Plaid Enterprises, Inc.
(800) 842-4197
www.plaidonline.com

Polar Bear Press
(801) 451-7670
www.polarbearpress.com

Prima Marketing, Inc.*
(909) 627-5532
www.primamarketinginc.com

Provo Craft
(800) 937-7686
www.provocraft.com

PSX Design
www.sierra-enterprises.com/psxmain.html

Punch Bunch, The
(254) 791-4209
www.thepunchbunch.com

Purple Onion Designs
www.purpleoniondesigns.com

Queen & Co.
(858) 613-7858
www.queenandcompany.com

QuicKutz, Inc.
(888) 702-1146
www.quickutz.com

Ranger Industries, Inc.*
(800) 244-2211
www.rangerink.com

Rouge de Garance
www.rougedegarance.com

Sanford Corporation
(800) 323-0749
www.sanfordcorp.com

Sassafras Lass
(801) 269-1331
www.sassafraslass.com

Scenic Route Paper Co.
(801) 542-8071
www.scenicroutepaper.com

ScrapArtist
(734) 717-7775
www.scrapartist.com

Scrapbook Adhesives by 3L*
www.scrapbook-adhesives.com

Scrapbook Graphics
www.scrapbookgraphics.com

Scrapbour
www.scrapbour.com

SEI, Inc.
(800) 333-3279
www.shopsei.com

Shabby Princess
www.shabbyprincess.com

Sharpie - see Sanford

Stampabilities
(800) 888-0321
www.stampabilities.com

Stampendous!
(800) 869-0474
www.stampendous.com

Stampin' Up!
(800) 782-6787
www.stampinup.com

Staples, Inc.
www.staples.com

Stemma/Masterpiece Studios
www.masterpiecestudios.com

Strano Designs
(508) 454-4615
www.stranodesigns.com

Sugarloaf Products, Inc.
(770) 484-0722
www.sugarloafproducts.com

Technique Tuesday, LLC
(503) 644-4073
www.techniquetuesday.com

Therm O Web, Inc.
(800) 323-0799
www.thermoweb.com

Tinkering Ink*
(877) 727-2784
www.tinkeringink.com

Tsukineko, Inc.
(800) 769-6633
www.tsukineko.com

Two Peas in a Bucket
(888) 896-7327
www.twopeasinabucket.com

Uniball/Sanford
(800) 323-0749
www.uniball-na.com

Upsy Daisy Designs*
www.upsydaisydesigns.com

Urban Lily
www.urbanlily.com

Village Impressions
www.villageimpressions.com

Wal-Mart Stores, Inc.
www.walmart.com

We R Memory Keepers, Inc.
(801) 539-5000
www.weronthenet.com

Westrim Crafts
(800) 727-2727
www.westrimcrafts.com

WorldWin Papers*
(888) 834-6455
www.worldwinpapers.com

Wrights Ribbon Accents
(877) 597-4448
www.wrights.com

Xyron
(800) 793-3523
www.xyron.com

Zingboom Kits
www.zingboomkits.com

Zsiage, LLC
(718) 224-1976
www.zsiage.com

125

INDEX

For more ways to cut loose, check out these other Memory Makers Books.

Flip, Spin & Play

Step-by-step instructions on a variety of techniques show you how to create engaging, interactive pages that beg to be touched.

ISBN-13: 978-1-59963-018-2
ISBN-10: 1-59963-018-4

paperback
128 pages
Z1679

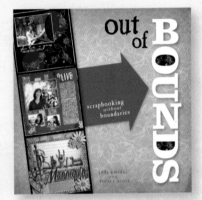

Out of Bounds

Push the boundaries of your scrapbooking with creative inspiration and innovative ideas from leading scrapbook designers Jodi Amidei and Torrey Scott.

ISBN-13: 978-1-59963-009-0
ISBN-10: 1-59963-009-5

paperback
128 pages
Z0795

See what's coming up from Memory Makers Books by checking out our blog:

www.mycraftivity.com/
scrapbooking_papercrafts/blog/

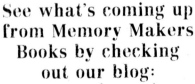

Scraptastic!

Ashley Calder shows you how to experiment with art supplies, try unfamiliar tools, and have fun making messy, sparkly, touchy-feely, snazzy scrapbook layouts.

ISBN-13: 978-1-59963-011-3
ISBN-10: 1-59963-011-7

paperback
128 pages
Z1007

We Dare You

Take your art to a new level and explore new themes with the mix of thoughtful, evocative and funny Dares from authors Kristina Contes, Meghan Dymock, Nisa Fiin and Genevieve Simmonds.

ISBN-13: 978-1-59963-013-7
ISBN-10: 1-59963-013-3

paperback
128 pages
Z1041

These books and other fine Memory Makers titles are available at your local scrapbook retailer, bookstore or from online suppliers, or visit our Web site at www.memorymakersmagazine.com or www.mycraftivity.com

SEP 72

group that includes Sandy, Cindy Lou, Harriet, Pi, and Chico. They looked into my eyes and connected with something deep inside. Each of them taught me something important about who I am, what I could do, and what we could do together.

I was lucky enough to have my parents with me for most of my career. They were able to see what I accomplished based on what they had taught me. They were there to support me in my low times. At first, it seemed very sad to me that my father died just days before I got the news that I would be receiving a Tony Honor. Then it became clear to me that my father was looking out for me and had sent me this gift. It gave me hope and the strength to move forward. When I accepted the award, I thanked the Tony committee, my wife and daughter, my staff, and all the rescue animals that have made me what I am today. But I dedicated the award to my father.

When you get gifts like that, you have to show your gratitude. That's why I'm donating 20 percent of my royalties to The Sandy Fund at the Humane Society of New York.

There's one other thing I've learned over my career, and it's something I hope you've learned from reading this book. There are great animals at your local shelter that need homes. All of the animals I've trained, including my superdogs, were rescues, animals that someone had abandoned or given up on. If you adopt a homeless animal, you may also find that special connection.

Adopt an animal, and you will find your own star.